Santa Fe Streamliners
The Chiefs and Their Tribesmen

by Karl Zimmermann

ISBN-0-915276-41-0

QUADRANT PRESS, INC.
19 West 44th Street
New York, N. Y. 10036
Phone: (212) 819-0822

Cover photograph: The *San Francisco Chief* highballs under threatening skies at Dalies, New Mexico.
PHOTO BY STEVE PATTERSON

With an all-lightweight consist, Santa Fe's *Chief* ascends Cajon Pass eastbound on November 28, 1947, behind a set of freight FT's converted for passenger service. STAN KISTLER

This book is for Mom, who took me West.

SANTA FE
INDIAN FLUTE
PULLMAN

1

Remembering the Super Chief

No. 18, the eastbound *Super Chief,* rounds a curve near Ribera, New Mexico, behind the combined muscle of five F-units. Fourth car from the front is the Pleasure Dome lounge, and directly behind that is the dining car. In the foreground is Pullman *Indian Flute,* one of twelve *Indian*-series 24-duplex-roomette cars built in 1947 by Pullman-Standard and rebuilt by Santa Fe in 1964 as 11-double-bedroom sleepers for *Super Chief* service. SANTA FE RAILWAY

Stepping out under the umbrella sheds at Los Angeles Union Passenger Terminal on an August evening in 1969 with my wife Laurel, I saw stretched before me a silver train, glimmering with allure in the half light of dusk. The windows of bedrooms and roomettes glowed cozily, promising rest and comfort, a home (albeit temporary) on the way to home. Up ahead, multiple diesel units, anxious to be off on their jaunt more than half way across the continent, chanted impatiently.

We passed by Pullmans—*Pine Beach, Indian Squaw, Regal Court*—until we reached our own. At the vestibule our porter, resplendent in dark-blue livery, waited to show us to our bedroom and help with our bags. No sooner had we settled in than we felt the gentle tug signaling the beginning of our 2,222-mile journey through the infinite variety of America.

This was the Santa Fe's final version of the *Super Chief,* even then a train worth talking about and easy to recommend. At a time when virtually all other passenger trains in the United States were a shambles, it remained clean, impeccably maintained, well staffed, and equipped in a reasonable equivalent of the grand manner through which it originally gained its fame.

The *Super Chief* had been synonymous with excellence ever since its inauguration in 1936 as a once-a-week, extra-fare, luxury heavyweight train. The *Super* was equipped the next year with cars in the then-new streamliner mode. In 1938 its frequency doubled, to twice weekly. In 1946 it was increased to every-other-day and in 1948 to daily. The equipment in use into the first years of the Amtrak era was introduced in 1950 and 1951 and received a major refurbishing in 1958. The train aged well and had a crisp, new feeling even when we rode in 1969. Right up until Amtrak took over two years later, Santa Fe offered *Super Chief* passengers convenience, courtesy, comfort, and a renewal of acquaintance with America.

The essential ingredient was the railroad's awareness that aesthetics are as important an element of travel as speed—though speed had been the *Super*'s original claim to fame. Getting from one place to the other is not for the civilized voyager the sole aim of travel; equally important is what happens along the way. On the *Super Chief,* "first class" continued to mean more than a few extra inches of seat.

The Santa Fe, like Kubla Khan, had decreed a "Pleasure Dome," which Pullman-Standard was pleased to supply back in 1950. This fine lounge car, borrowing both name and spirit from poet Samuel Taylor Coleridge, was luxurious and unusual. The main area was softly lighted and reminiscent of a tastefully furnished living room. It was just right for reading, watching the passing landscape, or engaging in conversation.

Under the dome was tucked a snug little cocktail bar, where a steward served expertly-mixed drinks—

Indian designs, heritage, and curios have for many decades been important to Santa Fe and The Fred Harvey Company, the railroad's partner in lunch room, dining car, and hotel operations from 1876 to 1969. Here, in the shadowy archway of the Indian Building at the Santa Fe station in Albuquerque, New Mexico — part of a complex that included Fred Harvey's Alvarado Hotel — an Indian woman peddles her wares. KARL ZIMMERMANN

no prepackaged cocktails here—as we watched the lights flickering on in houses along the way that first evening. We reveled in the fine sense of security that comes from being inside a train looking out at the world scrambling about its business. Adjacent to the bar was the car's most unusual feature—the Turquoise Room, for private dining. Wood-paneled and keynoted by a large turquoise medallion of southwestern Indian design, this handsome room could be reserved in advance by groups of six to ten. Well-iced, silver-bucketed champagne was no stranger here.

And then there was the dome itself. In the years since the mid-forties when Chicago, Burlington & Quincy had introduced the concept of the Vista-Dome, virtually every noteworthy western train with substantial daylight running in its schedule had come to carry in its consist some variation on this theme. The *Super Chief*'s car, however, had a unique feature. Rather than the usual four seats across the dome, there were only two, which revolved in parlor-car fashion. For comfort the entire car was, as Coleridge had it, ". . . a miracle of rare device, / A sunny pleasure dome. . . ."

Night had fallen over the California hills when we moved from the lounge into the diner. From the moment the waiter had passed through the train playing the dinner chimes until he brought our fluted silver finger bowls, we were constantly reminded that the great tradition of dining in transit yet survived—though its days decidedly were numbered. For those in an extravagant mood there was the "Champagne Dinner," a feast of shrimp cocktail and charcoal-broiled sirloin. Other dinners included mountain trout and filet mignon with sauce bernaise.

Santa Fe stinted in no way. Service was on handsome, distinctive Mimbreno china, designed for the 1937 *Super*. Each piece bore a different Indian pictograph. In the bud vases were God's own roses, sweet-smelling and fresh. The waiters were skillful and attentive, still anxious to please.

Although Santa Fe's route is less spectacular than those of the more northerly transcontinentals, we did get a fine feeling of the vastness of the West. The railroad had long been alert to the aesthetics of American Indian art, and the southwestern terrain outside appropriately complemented the interior design. On

Above, the *Super Chief* winds through Apache Canyon, near Lamy, New Mexico. Top right, a feast featuring broiled African lobster tails, fresh asparagus, and well-chilled champagne is arranged on silver and Mimbreno china. Bottom right, a Pullman room at night is a remarkably cozy nest.
SANTA FE RAILWAY

Welcome
aboard the

SUPER CHIEF

We are delighted to have you aboard the Super Chief, and want you to enjoy to the fullest extent its many services and facilities that are briefly described in this leaflet.

It is our aim to make the Super Chief a train you'll always remember, providing the type of service you'll never forget.

Issued June 8, 19

Top, the eastbound *Super Chief*'s "Pleasure Dome" stands ready to receive passengers at Los Angeles Union Passenger Terminal prior to the train's evening departure. Bottom, one of the car's features was the Turquoise Room for private dining. SANTA FE RAILWAY

the first afternoon out we were treated to the line's finest scenery. New Mexico's rugged Apache Canyon was barely by when we began the ascent to Raton Pass, the highest point on the railroad. More important than any particular view, however, was the sense of movement and ever-changing landscape which provided a spiritual continuity with our westering forebears.

Somewhere here is grounded the *Super Chief* mystique, the reason why crossing the continent in its cars was such a wonderful experience. Scenery, service, food, equipment, and cachet were all elements of its magic—but even in sum were not a full explanation. Somehow there was a thrill in eating up the miles, in watching America blur by, in being aware of every mountain range or river. Then, too, there was the sense of the rightness of things, the gracious but not ostentatious luxury of an all-room train—which the *Super* was during peak Christmas travel seasons and for one last summer in 1969—the last such remaining. Travel aboard the *Super Chief* appealed to all the sensibilities, not just to the stopwatch.

In retrospect, perhaps the greatest miracle of all was that the Santa Fe maintained its flagship with such impeccable spit and polish right up to the very threshold of Amtrak, allowing travelers who came to it late to sense encapsulated the rich and fascinating history of the thirty-five years' worth of stainless-steel streamliners that led to this last great statement—the final *Super Chief*.

Left, as the westbound *Super* makes its curving ascent of Raton Pass in southern Colorado, the dome is packed with sightseers. Right, the train speeds past the Devil's Footstool, near Los Cerrillos, New Mexico. SANTA FE RAILWAY

2 Predecessors

The Santa Fe tradition of luxury varnish goes back a long way, witness the broad-windowed parlor car with open observation platform carrying the markers for this short consist making a station stop. OTTO C. PERRY, DENVER PUBLIC LIBRARY, WESTERN HISTORY COLLECTION

Think Santa Fe passenger service and certain images and associations probably leap to mind: movie stars and moguls, fluted stainless steel, Fred Harvey diners, the Southwest, Indian motifs and aesthetics, the colorful "warbonnet" paint scheme wrapped around Electro-Motive diesel snouts, extra-fare all-Pullman luxury, Chicago's Dearborn Station and Los Angeles Union Passenger Terminal. Though many of these touchstones were unique to the dash and dazzle of the streamliner era, others predated it by more than half a century. Santa Fe's explosion of streamliners in the late thirties did not ignite in a vacuum. These trains were an extension, albeit a flamboyant and radical one, of a tradition of passenger carriage that dated back to the early 1870's and of true luxury service from as far back as 1892.

The *California Limited* was inaugurated then, as Santa Fe's Chicago-Los Angeles flagship on a year-round schedule. Fred Harvey had begun operating dining cars on Santa Fe varnish in 1888, and the *California Limited* carried one between Fort Madison, Iowa, and Kansas City, stopping at Harvey Houses for meals over the balance of the route. This incarnation of the *California Limited* was discontinued on May 3, 1896—to be reborn the following winter as a seasonal, biweekly, all-Pullman luxury service, covering what was then a route of 2,265 miles between Chicago and Los Angeles in seventy-two hours. This train, which became year-round in 1900 and daily in 1905, remained the road's premier service until December 11, 1911, when a truly extraordinary successor hit the rails.

This was the *Santa Fe de-Luxe,* perhaps the most exclusive, opulent, and elegant railroad passenger service ever offered in America. A winter season weekly train, the *de-Luxe* could accommodate no more than sixty passengers—its six-car consist included a diner, club car (with smoking room, barber shop, and shower), and 10-section observation-parlor, for a very high proportion of non-revenue space—and commanded a whopping extra fare of $25. For this substantial surcharge, the first ever for a Chicago-California service, the passenger could sleep in a brass bed rather than a berth; borrow books from the library in the observation parlor; enjoy savory Fred Harvey meals in a 30-seat dining car decorated with vermillion mahogany and kept comfortable by the first "air-cooling and air-washing device" ever installed in a rail vehicle; receive, if a woman, an orchid corsage brought aboard near the California border by a flower boy or, if a man, an alligator wallet embossed in gold with the train's name (customs begun aboard the 1896 *California Limited*).

Postwar years brought the inauguration of another extra-fare, all-Pullman service and the first use of the name that would come to be emblematic of Santa Fe's passenger operations in the lightweight era: the *Chief*.

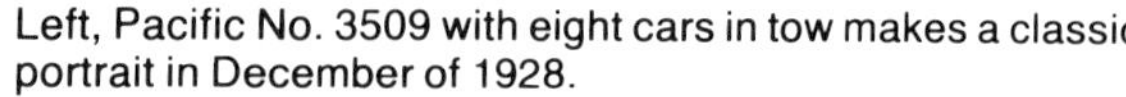

Left, Pacific No. 3509 with eight cars in tow makes a classic portrait in December of 1928.

Remaining on the 63-hour schedule instituted by the *de-Luxe,* the first *Chief* began operation on September 14, 1926, as a daily service requiring an extra fare of $10. Soon it became the darling of the burgeoning and glamorous film industry—a glittering association that was instrumental in keeping it and later the *Super Chief* in the media spotlight.

Of course, not all Santa Fe varnish had such pretensions to luxury. At the other end of the spectrum—though excellent in its own modest way, as might be expected from Santa Fe—was the Los Angeles-Chicago *Scout,* inaugurated on January 16, 1916, and serving from the Depression years onward as an economy train on the route through Amarillo, Texas, known as the "Southern District." The *Scout* carried a car reserved for women and children and offered the services of a courier-nurse with these publics in mind. In 1936, when the big passenger news at Santa Fe was the inauguration of the heavyweight *Super Chief,* the railroad's Topeka Shops provided a consist of rebuilt standard equipment for the *Scout,* sporting two-tone gray paint and carrying nameboards.

Then there was the *Grand Canyon Limited,* a train for tourists with through Pullmans to that American mecca. This train, which remained heavyweight far into the lightweight era (though with temporary forays into streamlining), began service in 1929. Basically a Chicago-Los Angeles service, at one time or another it sent through Pullmans on to Oakland, Phoenix, Galveston, Denver, and Houston—as well as the South Rim of the Grand Canyon.

In its first year, the *Grand Canyon Limited* participated in a unique experiment, short-lived but, in the light of later events, monumentally significant. To cut New York City-Los Angeles travel time from one hundred to eighty hours, Santa Fe, the Pennsylvania Railroad, and Curtiss Aeroplane Company sponsored a combined air-rail service: Pullman by night, Ford Tri-motor by day. The legs were these: New York City to Columbus, Ohio, on the Pennsy; to Waynoka, Oklahoma, by Transcontinental Air Transport; to Clovis, New Mexico, by Santa Fe's *Grand Canyon Limited;* and on to Los Angeles by Transcontinental Air.

There were, of course, many other trains too, short or long-haul, short or long-lived. The Chicago-California *Navajo* was almost twenty-five years old when it was withdrawn in 1939 in favor of the new streamliners. The *Ranger* provided service to Galveston for a decade longer, through the forties. But it is in the lineage of the *Santa Fe de-Luxe* and the *Chief*—all-Pullman, "extra fare, extra fast, extra fine" heavyweights—that the heritage of the *Super Chief,* Santa Fe's prototypical streamliner, can be found.

In this evolution there was no missing link, for a temporary, heavyweight *Super Chief* in 1936 bridged the gap between the deluxe services that were an important part of Santa Fe history and the streamliner fleet that lay in the future. However excellent, that first, heavyweight *Super Chief* (its Pullmans, diner, and club car just spiffed-up members of the *Chief* pool) was not revolutionary in consist and service. In fact, it traded on the superb reputation already established by the *Chief.* What *was* revolutionary was its speed, for the *Super* would cut an extraordinary 15 hours and 15 minutes from the *Chief*'s eastbound timing, bringing it below the magic 40-hour mark, to 39 hours and 45 minutes. Revolutionary too, not coincidentally, was the motive power.

These "Phostint" post cards, made by Detroit Publishing Company for Fred Harvey, convey some of the many moods of pre-streamliner passenger railroading on the Santa Fe.

Left, in the days before streamliners, an open observation platform and drumhead — such as adorn the Chicago-Los Angeles *Scout* in this view — where *de rigueur* for any train of quality. Middle, there is no shortage of activity in this photograph of the interior of the *Scout*'s heavyweight lounge. The couple at the far right studies a brochure of the Grand Canyon; a mother with her daughter in her lap works at the writing desk; a steward serves patrons seated in the four sections in the background. Barely visible through the door all the way to the rear is a woman — most likely a courier-nurse — dandling a baby on her knee. Right, throughout the twentieth century the Grand Canyon has proven a magnet for tourists — and thus a great traffic generator for Santa Fe. Here, on January 4, 1936, a sea of Pullmans — including *Pericles,* in the foreground — fills the yard at the South Rim of the Grand Canyon. A Southern Methodist University special is in the station. LEFT AND MIDDLE, SANTA FE RAILWAY: RIGHT, ROBERT J. WAYNER COLLECTION

By the middle years of the Depression-ridden thirties, streamlining was the talk of railroading, providing a much-needed psychological lure intended to revive flagging passenger loadings. Union Pacific with its M-10000 and Burlington with its *Zepyhr* had led the charge in early 1934, and some other railroads had followed along quickly: Milwaukee Road with its *Hiawathas*, Baltimore & Ohio with the *Royal Blue* and *Abraham Lincoln,* New York, New Haven & Hartford with the *Comet,* Gulf, Mobile & Northern with the *Rebel,* and Illinois Central with the *Green Diamond.*

Though Santa Fe was not in the vanguard of streamlining, thoughtful consideration and planning had been going on as long at AT&SF as at other roads. At Santa Fe's Chicago headquarters, two premises had become clear. First, the railroad was not interested in undersized, permanently coupled trainsets. Santa Fe wanted full-sized equipment, not "toys," and it wanted the flexibility of individual, autonomous cars. Second, when Santa Fe planners—in particular John Purcell, superintendent of motive power—looked at the arid deserts through which their lines ran in Arizona and New Mexico, they embraced the idea of dieselization to end the need to haul water into these areas for steam locomotives. This was a daring decision, for at that time the diesel was almost completely untried in road service.

As a result Santa Fe ordered pioneering road diesels to power the first *Super Chief.* Carrying road numbers 1 and 1A, they had engines from Electro-Motive Corporation and carbodies from St. Louis Car Company. Each unit had two 900-horsepower Winton diesels, for a total of 3,600 horsepower for the two units, which were intended to be run as a pair. The locomotives were designed by Richard Dilworth, EMC's chief engineer, and were nearly identical to EMC demonstrators Nos. 511 and 512, which had been built in May 1935, just four months ahead of AT&SF Nos. 1 and 1A, which appeared in September. (Baltimore & Ohio No. 50, another sister, hit the rails in August.) In spite of being delivered in the streamlined era, these units were basically just flat-faced box cabs—with, in the case of Santa Fe's locomotives, hulking "eyebrow" cowls containing air intakes looming over those faces, doing nothing to help appearances.

One thing that was modern about these bulky box-cabs was a snappy paint scheme—cobalt blue roof, Saratoga blue undercarriage, olive green body, with separating stripes of scarlet and Tuscan red. This combination was the work of Sterling McDonald, a Chicago industrial designer who had done the interiors for the DC-3 aircraft. For this first *Super* he also provided the locomotive's illuminated nose sign and the observation-car drumhead. For the second *Super,* he would provide much more.

"Amos 'n' Andy" the AT&SF's new diesels were called, after the radio team; they ran extensive tests all over the system with generally excellent results, though No. 1 did go back to Electro-Motive for rebuilding after catching fire. In particular, a preliminary Chicago-Los Angeles run of the *Super Chief* was made November 19-21, 1935, proving the impossible dream of a 39-hour 45-minute schedule to be achievable.

Thus on Tuesday, May 12, 1936, the *Super Chief* was officially born—as a diesel-powered, all-Pullman, weekly, extra-fare ($10, the same as the *Chief*), heavyweight train that brought Chicago and Los Angeles within one business day of each other.

The name "Super Chief" seems so apt and natural that it's surprising and often amusing to look back at alternatives which were suggested and rejected: Big Chief, Far West Limited, Cactus Special, Westward Ho, Victory Limited, Elite Special, The Franciscan, Stars Limited, Hollywood Limited, Sunstate Special, Redwood Special, Sunbound Special, Redman Special, Chieftain, Flash, Blue Streak, and a number of others.

The service bore numbers 17 and 18, which would remain the *Super*'s throughout its Santa Fe career. That inaugural train left Chicago's Dearborn Station at 7:15 p.m. and arrived the day after next at La Grande Station in Los Angeles one minute early at 8:59 a.m.

Left, daughter sleeps with shades down, mother reads with shades up, in a cozy scene circa 1930. Right, pioneering "Amos 'n' Andy" diesels Nos. 1 and 1A for the heavyweight *Super Chief.* SANTA FE RAILWAY

To accomplish this, "Amos 'n' Andy" cranked up to 102 miles an hour at one point. On Friday, May 15, the *Super* made its first eastbound departure at 8 p.m. arriving Chicago on Sunday at 1:38 p.m., seven minutes early.

Naturally, great hoopla attended this round trip. Celebrities aboard for the westbound jaunt included Mrs. Eddie Cantor and Eleanor Powell. There was a radio broadcast over station WGN. Samuel T. Bledsoe, Santa Fe's president, took a leading role, and it was his daughter, Mrs. Bartlett Cormack, who broke a bottle of California champagne over the flower-bedecked railing of *Crystal View,* the *Super*'s 3-compartment 2-drawing-room-observation-lounge. As it happened, May 12 was his birthday, lending an extra resonance to the festivities. This was certainly appropriate, since Bledsoe had been instrumental in the creation not only of the heavyweight *Super Chief* but also of the long-planned lightweight fleet already abuilding at the Edward G. Budd Manufacturing Company in Philadelphia.

3

A Super Train

The lounge *Acoma,* built by Budd for the 1937 lightweight *Super Chief,* surely featured one of the most exquisite interiors that ever rode the rails. Zebrawood paneling dominated the decor. A striking Navajo design graced the backbar, flanked by small Indian vases. SANTA FE RAILWAY

"Super" is the ultimate superlative, and to no train could it more justly be applied than to the lightweight *Super Chief* of 1937—the genuine article for which the 1936 heavyweight version had been just a temporary stand-in. Many factors, and the work of many talented individuals, came together to make this train among the most beautiful ever, anywhere.

From the heavyweight *Super* the 1937 train inherited its name and once-a-week, 39-hour 45-minute schedule; from it and other Santa Fe predecessors came the celebrity among celebrities, the tradition of deluxe, the exquisite excellence of the Fred Harvey diner. On the other hand, the physical consist had no lineal ancestors, being truly innovative both mechanically and aesthetically. From stem to stern it looked like this: slant- and smooth-nosed Electro-Motive E1A No. 2 in red and yellow "warbonnet" paint scheme, followed by E1B No. 2A; then eight shiny Budd-built cars of fluted stainless steel. They were baggage car 3430, 8-section 1-drawing-room 2-compartment sleeper *Isleta,* 6-double-bedroom 2-compartment 2-drawing-room sleeper *Taos,* dormitory-barber shop-buffet lounge *Acoma,* 36-seat diner *Cochiti,* a second 6-2-2 sleeper *Oraibi,* a second 8-1-2 sleeper *Laguna,* and 2-drawing-room 1-double-bedroom 3-compartment lounge-observation *Navajo,* carrying the purple *Super Chief* drumhead.

Though it was the interiors of these cars that caused the greatest comment at the time—and in the long run have proven their claim to fame—those gleaming exteriors, their appearance endlessly replicated by various builders for many railroads in the years since the *Super*'s inaugural, were worthy of comment too. They were assembled by "Shotwelding," a patented procedure invented by Colonel E. J. W. Ragsdale, the chief engineer of Budd's railway division. In an article for *The Santa Fe Magazine,* Ragsdale eloquently summed up the not inconsiderable virtues of stainless steel equipment: "These cars not only have a bright, enduring finish, but they are lighter, stronger, and more economical of operation. For once, a brilliant appearance can be combined with a definite utility."

Shotwelding involves the passage of a measured "shot" of electricity through stainless steel, melting together touching surfaces but leaving exterior surfaces unaltered. The current is so strong and the time so short that the strength of the metal is preserved and harmful carbide precipitation avoided. A weld recorder constantly monitors the process, writing on a paper tape and ringing warning bells if a weld fails.

The Shotweld process was introduced with the Chicago, Burlington & Quincy's *Zephyr* in 1934. This was a permanently coupled trainset, with cars smaller than the heavyweights they replaced. The pioneering standard-sized stainless-steel passenger car was Santa

Fe's No. 3070, delivered in January 1936 from Budd, the first of its kind built for any railroad. This experimental car, operated all over the Santa Fe in a thorough trial, was the progenitor of all the streamlined *Chiefs* which followed—and countless stainless-steel trains on other railroads as well.

Shotwelded, this deluxe coach introduced many of the design features that would be refined in the all-Pullman *Super Chief* of 1937. Most obvious was the fluted stainless-steel exterior. The car weighted just 83,000 pounds, compared to a then "conventional," or heavyweight, car's 160,000 pounds, but was more spacious inside. The coach featured heavy insulation, air conditioning, hermetically sealed double panes of glass in large windows, and an interior dominated by various elegant wood veneers. No. 3070 proved an unqualified success, bringing to Budd the order for the first lightweight *Super;* the car remained in regular service into the 1980's, ending its days hauling commuters for NJ Transit.

Two other lightweight experimentals tested on the Santa Fe. In November of 1936, No. 3071 was delivered from St. Louis Car Company. Like 3070, it contained just fifty-two seats (as opposed to eighty aboard the standard heavyweights), with substantial space at each end for men's and women's lounges. In features and interior decor, 3071 was roughly similar to 3070, but the St. Louis coach was constructed of Corten steel and weighed in at 98,000 pounds, substantially more than Budd's Shotwelded stainless-steel car.

The first lightweight Pullman to operate on the Santa Fe was the 8-section 2-double-bedroom 2-compartment *Forward,* built by Pullman-Standard in November of 1936 for the Pullman pool. It was, in fact, the first conventional-sized streamlined sleeper built; it spent many of its early days in the consist of the otherwise-heavyweight *Super Chief. Forward,* which had a fluted stainless-steel outer skin, was the first car built with Corten steel truss frames, the construction principle used in steel curtain-wall skyscrapers. (Santa Fe bought *Forward* from Pullman in 1948 and rebuilt it into baggage-dorm 3437 in 1963.)

But by the time these St. Louis Car and Pullman-Standard experimentals hit Santa Fe iron, the railroad had already chosen The Edward G. Budd Manufacturing Company to build its first lightweight streamliner: the incomparable *Super Chief* of 1937. Budd and Santa Fe proved wonderfully productive design partners, along with Electro-Motive, which supplied the diesels. Among these participants, a virtual army of creative people was marshalled to achieve a once-only aesthetic triumph. On April 7, 1936, at a meeting of Budd and Santa Fe personnel at Budd's Red Lion Plant in Philadelphia, the project was begun. A week later the sales order was signed.

Sterling B. McDonald, a designer-decorator with a studio in Chicago's Merchandise Mart, had been spotted by Santa Fe for his work on the first two brown-and-yellow Union Pacific *Streamliners* and given the assignment of designing the successful diesel paint scheme for the heavyweight *Super Chief.* To him would fall substantial responsibility for the conception of the exquisite interiors aboard the streamlined *Super.* Southwestern Indian art would supply the basic aesthetic, continuing a direction already established by Santa Fe in decor and advertising. Roger W. Birdseye, Santa Fe's general advertising manager and an expert in Indian culture, lent his substantial knowledge. (Among other things, he would select the names for the

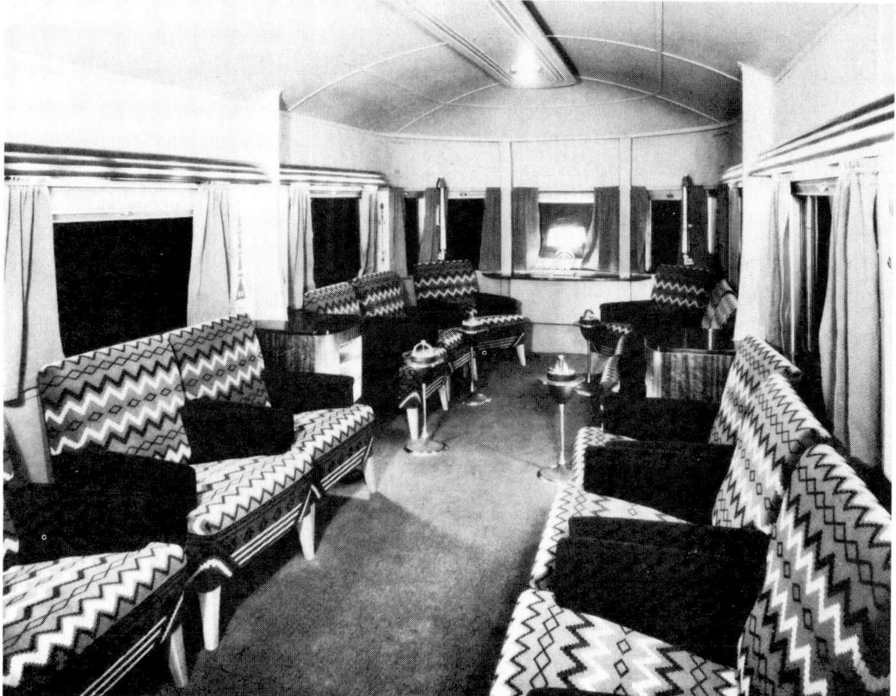

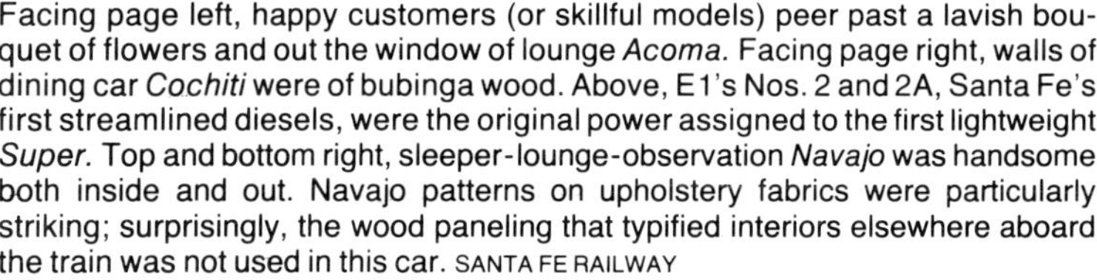
Facing page left, happy customers (or skillful models) peer past a lavish bouquet of flowers and out the window of lounge *Acoma.* Facing page right, walls of dining car *Cochiti* were of bubinga wood. Above, E1's Nos. 2 and 2A, Santa Fe's first streamlined diesels, were the original power assigned to the first lightweight *Super.* Top and bottom right, sleeper-lounge-observation *Navajo* was handsome both inside and out. Navajo patterns on upholstery fabrics were particularly striking; surprisingly, the wood paneling that typified interiors elsewhere aboard the train was not used in this car. SANTA FE RAILWAY

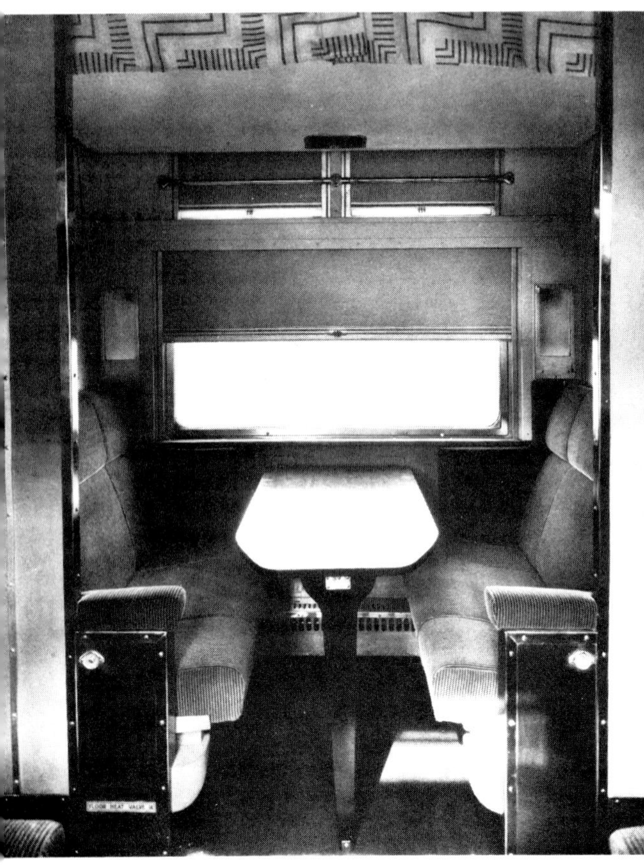

cars.) McDonald's sketches of the car interiors provided direction for a pair of skilled and creative Budd architects, Paul Philippe Cret and John Harbeson.

Cret was dean of the University of Pennsylvania's School of Architecture and Harbeson a professor there. What they were to do with this *Super Chief* was unprecedented and remains unparalleled. Santa Fe had asked for nine nonarticulated standard-sized cars to sleep 104 passengers and house a dining-car crew of twelve. The railroad envisioned an RPO-mail storage (ordered but subsequently eliminated, reducing the consist size to eight), a mail-baggage, five sleepers, a diner, and a full lounge containing crew quarters and a barber's room. Each of the seven passenger-carrying cars was to be a unique self-contained design unit, with no two alike—a remarkably ambitious undertaking, particularly considering that exotic woods were to be employed virtually throughout.

The secret to this use of rare and beautiful woods was Flexwood Veneer, specified by Harbeson. This was a thin layer of real wood mounted on a muslin backing, applied over masonite siding. Bubinga, white harewood, macassar ebony, ribbon primavera, zebrawood, Brazilian rosewood, ebonized maple, American holly, redwood burl, teak, aspen, and satinwood: all these were used in the *Super Chief* interiors. Each of the thirty-two double bedrooms, compartments, and drawing rooms was finished in a unique combination of fabric and wood, with no two alike. *The Santa Fe Magazine* boasted, not without justification, that "the change from the heavy, dark oppressiveness of the uniformly finished Pullmans of yesterday is delightful."

Acoma, the lounge car, was done primarily in zebrawood, while *Cochiti*, the diner, had walls of bubinga wood. The observation-lounge section aboard *Navajo*, curiously, did not use wood but was striking nonetheless. Appropriately, Navajo designs were the keynote, with upholstery of a dramatic fabric that was an accurate reproduction of native weaving. The carpeting was the color of desert sands, the lower walls of copper hue, and the ceiling turquoise. On the pier panels between windows were authentic copies of sand paintings illustrating the "Myth of the Mountains" chant. (*Acoma*'s cocktail lounge also used Navajo art: in its backbar ornamentation, rug, and sacred sand paintings adorning the lamps.)

Design planning went beyond the cars themselves. Mary Colter created a unique china exclusively for use aboard *Cochiti*. An artist, designer, and architect employed by Fred Harvey and Santa Fe and an authority on Indians of the Southwest, she was particularly fascinated by the ornamented pottery of the small and ancient Mimbres tribe. Their designs—characterized by precisely drawn lines and geometric and checkered patterns in elaborate depictions of animals, in red on buff or white—were remarkable in that they remained essentially unchanged from 900 to 1200 A. D. The superb potters of the Mimbres tribe didn't borrow or modify designs; rather, they accurately reproduced the original versions through the centuries. Miss Colter recreated thirty-seven authentic motifs on the china she designed for the *Super Chief* and called "Mimbreno." This pattern, each piece adorned with a different pictograph, would be used throughout the life of the *Super Chief* and become perhaps the most famous of all dining-car crockery.

From the delicate design of china to the paint scheme of the pair of rugged Electro-Motive Corporation diesels that would power the first streamlined *Super Chief*, the aesthetics were exquisite. In carbody shape, EMC's slant-nosed, sleek E1A No. 2 and E1B No. 2A represented a new world of futuristic grace when compared to the boxy if seviceable pioneers 1 and 1A. And to adorn this elegant shape, Leland A. Knickerbocker, an Electro-Motive illustrator, provided what would become the best-known diesel paint scheme ever: the famous "warbonnet," built around

Top left, wood was used even in this ladies' rest room aboard the first streamlined *Super Chief*. Bottom left, note the upper berth windows — with shades down — in this view of a *Super* section. Facing page, the "warbonnet," the most famous of diesel paint schemes, was first worn by the 1937 *Super Chief*'s E1's. SANTA FE RAILWAY

SANTA FE

the profile of an Indian with headress feathers trailing.

Further, Knickerbocker modified the traditional round Santa Fe herald to an oval shape, stretching it out to fit gracefully across the E1's slanted nose. Like the Mimbreno china, his dazzling red, yellow, and silver paint scheme would last throughout the *Super Chief*'s Santa Fe career, adorning all of the countless diesels that would haul the *Super* and its lesser tribesmen.

By the spring of 1937, all these creative energies—of Knickerbocker, of Ragsdale, Cret, and Harbeson of the Budd Company, of Colter, Birdseye, McDonald, and President Samuel Bledsoe of Santa Fe—had produced a masterpiece (though diesels 2 and 2A were not ready yet). On April 28 the consist was put through its initial paces in a trial run in Philadelphia; the next day the cars headed for Chicago in the consist of the Pennsylvania Railroad's *Commercial Express*. A series of exhibition runs followed.

At 9 a.m. on Monday, May 3, with seventy-two passengers aboard—Santa Fe and Budd Company officials, along with newspaper and magazine editors and writers—the *Super Chief* left Chicago's Dearborn Station for Santa Fe, New Mexico. On the point was a steam locomotive, since the E1's hadn't yet been delivered. Arrival at Santa Fe was at 11:30 a.m. on May 4 and departure at 8:15 a.m. on May 6. In the interim, passengers enjoyed socializing and sightseeing, including a day of trips into Indian country (during which time the local populace was invited to inspect the temporarily empty consist).

A second preview trip—with spanking new warbonnet E1's now in charge—departed Chicago at 8:15 p.m. on May 8 with a delegation from the Chicago

"California Bound! The *Super Chief* departure from Dearborn Station, Chicago, is an occasion of interest and excitement," this painting was captioned. Used in the earliest publicity for the train, it became a staple feature in *Super Chief* brochures over a period spanning three decades. Though it features what must be observation *Navajo* — among all *Super Chief* and *Chief* sleeper-observations, the only one built by Budd, readily recognizable by a rounded boat-tail blunter than on Pullman-Standard cars — the painting was used long after *Navajo* was demoted from *Super* service and steam locomotives had vanished from Dearborn. SANTA FE RAILWAY

Association of Commerce aboard, bound for Los Angeles at the invitation of that city's chamber of commerce. Arrival at Los Angeles's La Grande Station at 8:58 a.m. on May 10—two minutes early—was greeted by a crowd of about three thousand. Welcoming ceremonies were broadcast over KFI, key station of the National Broadcasting chain. "Superspeed, superservice, and supercomfort" were the encomiums from the cartoonist John T. McCutcheon. "A necklace of pearls," said the announcer in an apt metaphor describing the stainless-steel consist. That evening the press was invited aboard for a preview party.

On Tuesday and Wednesday the train was exhibited in Los Angeles, and on Thursday in San Diego, where thirteen thousand visitors boarded. On Friday the *Super* returned to L. A., with San Diego business leaders and newspapermen aboard. (Already in the works at Budd in Philadelphia and EMC in La Grange were six more stainless-steel cars and another E1 locomotive that in less than a year would enter service on this route as the Santa Fe's *San Diegan*.)

On Saturday, May 15, at 8 p.m., the *Super* left Los Angeles with seventy important Californians aboard. When this final good-will trip ended at Dearborn Station at 11:48 a.m. on Monday, May 17, the *Super Chief* and its pair of E1 diesels had set a new speed record for the run from Los Angeles to Chicago: 36 hours and 49 minutes, two hours faster than the existing best, for an average of 60.8 miles per hour figured on the basis of total elapsed time, and 63.9 miles per hour in actual running time. The fastest dash came between La Junta, Colorado, and Dodge City, Kansas, with the *Super* covering 202 miles in 139 minutes, for an average speed of 87.2 miles an hour.

This record was not set without cost, however, for in their sprint the E1's had burned out a traction motor. Thus when the *Super Chief* entered regular once-a-week service the next day—May 18, 1937, a big date in passenger train annals—on the point were a boxy pair—Santa Fe's No. 1A (in aluminum paint with scarlet stripes, more compatible with the streamliner's stainless steel than the locomotive's original colorful dress) and EMC demonstrator No. 512 (in unadorned aluminum paint). This motive-power substitution was but a short-lived embarrassment which caused no inconvenience to the passengers, who from the beginning found the appointments and service aboard this first all-Pullman diesel-powered streamliner incomparable. Nor was the excitement dampened when, the very next day, Union Pacific inaugurated its own Chicago-L. A. streamliner, the *City of Los Angeles,* also on a 39-hour, 45-minute schedule. (In fact, Santa Fe and UP had an agreement to operate their premier streamliners on equal schedules.)

The inaugural lightweight *Super* — seen here into the second day of its journey, speeding west near Trinidad, Colorado, on May 19, 1937 — was powered by Santa Fe's No. 1A and EMC demonstrator No. 512. The intended elegance of E1's was temporarily deferred by a traction-motor burn-out suffered during a preview run. OTTO C. PERRY, DENVER PUBLIC LIBRARY, AMERICAN HISTORY COLLECTION

Even before the streamlined *Super Chief* ran its first mile, sister consists were far along in planning: a stainless-steel, warbonneted explosion which in the next year and a half would double the *Super*'s frequency, give it an all-coach running mate, streamline the existing daily *Chief,* and bring this new mode of rail travel to three additional routes. This replication and expansion was exciting and commendable but by its very nature spelled the end of the one-of-a-kind customization found in the design of that first streamlined *Super Chief.* That consist was a "string of pearls" indeed—but each pearl had its own unique luster, its own peculiar beauty. In the period of rapid growth that would follow, such custom design would be out of the question.

3460 3460
SANTA FE

4 Proliferation

On February 11 and 12, 1938, Chicago's Dearborn Station was the scene of great excitement as more than 30,000 visitors came to view the Santa Fe's new transcontinental streamliners. Here, E1 and E1A Nos. 3A and 3B are at the far left, on the point of the second streamlined *Super Chief* consist; next is "Blue Goose" Hudson No. 3460 with the *Chief*; at the right are E1's 5 and 6 with the two short *El Capitan* consists needed to inaugurate a twice-weekly Chicago-Los Angeles schedule for this coach streamliner, paralleling the *Super*'s Pullman-only service. SANTA FE RAILWAY

When 1937 ended, the first lightweight *Super Chief* was still a solo act, all by itself in the spotlight. But by 1940, quite a cast of supporting characters had joined it. There were, in fact, a total of seventeen Santa Fe streamliner consists in glittering stainless steel where just three years earlier there had been but one.

Proliferation of this kind had been part of President Bledsoe's plan from the very beginning. The record-setting speeds of the *Super Chief*—eastbound, more than fifteen hours faster than the previously hottest *Chief*—had been made possible by right-of-way improvements costing more than $4.5 million: hundreds of miles of new 112-pound rail, reballasting, straightening and superelevation of curves, and new signaling. This investment naturally looked better the more high-speed streamliners there were to travel these newly improved trails.

Therefore, in rapid succession came six streamlined consists for the existing Chicago-Los Angeles *Chief,* a second set of *Super Chief* cars to allow twice-weekly service, two luxury all-coach consists to inaugurate the twice-weekly *El Capitan* between Chicago and Los Angeles, a five-car train to make two daily Los Angeles-San Diego round trips as the *San Diegan,* two consists to run as the *Chicagoan* eastbound and *Kansas Cityan* westbound between those cities, two consists to run between Bakersfield, California, and San Francisco as the *Golden Gate,* a train to operate from Kansas City to Tulsa, Oklahoma, as the *Tulsan,* and, finally, a second *San Diegan* consist to allow four round trips daily.

Except for the *Chief,* which would be hauled by "Blue Goose" Hudson No. 3460 and her five unstreamlined sisters, all of these streamliners would be powered by graceful warbonneted Electro-Motive E-units: E1A's Nos. 2-9 and E1B's Nos. 2A-4A, delivered between June 1937 and April 1938, and E3's 11 and 11A, which arrived in 1939.

Budd was initially the Santa Fe's primary partner in streamliner planning. Conceived by AT&SF at the very beginning, along with the first stainless-steel *Super Chief,* was a six-car *El Capitan* and a six-car *San Diegan*. In addition, even before the first *Super* had been delivered, AT&SF had placed a major order with Budd for cars to streamline existing trains: ten diners, six club lounge-dormitories, and six baggage-barber shop-buffet lounges, all for the *Chief,* and thirty deluxe coaches, intended for the *Scout* (an economy tourist train) but turning up in other service as well. These were all delivered in 1937, giving the Santa Fe the largest fleet of stainless-steel cars at the time, ahead of even the Chicago, Burlington & Quincy, which with its *Zephyr* had been the first railroad to operate such equipment.

The *Scout,* an economy Chicago-Los Angeles service that dates back to 1916, in 1936 received heavyweight consists refurbished in the railroad's Topeka Shops, painted in a two-tone gray scheme and carrying distinctive nameboards on car sides below the windows. In 1937, lightweight stainless-steel coaches from a thirty-car order from Budd were added. They are visible in these views, both taken in 1941 of No. 2, the eastbound *Scout,* at Nelson, Arizona. D. L. INGERSOLL, GORDON C. BASSETT COLLECTION

Other orders to Budd followed soon on the heels of this major one—orders for diners, coaches, lounges, and parlors to equip the coach streamliners *El Capitan, San Diegan, Chicagoan, Kansas Cityan, Golden Gate* and *Tulsan*. In fact, virtually without exception the first fleet of streamliners relied on Budd for these types of cars. On the other hand, after the first lightweight *Super Chief,* AT&SF went just as single-mindedly to Pullman-Standard for its sleeping cars—presumably because of The Pullman Company's unwillingness to operate cars of other builders in those days before the antitrust action of 1947 split Pullman's carbuilding and operating arms. In the early years of Santa Fe streamlining, this amounted to orders for fifty-seven sleepers—all bearing Indian names—to streamline the *Chief* and add a second *Super Chief*.

On January 31, 1938, the *Chief*—Nos. 19 and 20, the daily, all-Pullman, extra-fare, Chicago-Los Angeles service instituted back in 1926—went lightweight, though it remained steam-hauled. This magnificent train would have been the flagship of virtually any other railroad's passenger-train fleet but on the Santa Fe was second to the *Super*. The *Chief*'s consist included a baggage-barber shop-buffet lounge, dormitory-club lounge, and 36-seat diner, along with seven Pullmans—clearly a first-class assemblage of equipment. (In fact, early promotional brochures featured the *Chief* and *Super Chief* jointly, making no distinction in equipment or services between the two.) The *Chief*'s seven sleepers were two 8-section 2-compartment 2-double-bedroom cars, two 4-compartment 2-drawing-room 4-double-bedroom cars, one 14-section car, and one 17-roomette car. Carrying the markers was a 4-drawing-room 1-double-bedroom lounge-observation: *Betahtakin, Biltabito, Chaistla, Chuska, Coconino,* or *Denehotso*.

The *Chiefs* were unique among Santa Fe's growing lightweight fleet in two ways: They were existing trains, and they remained steam-powered. East of La Junta, Colorado, the locomotives usually assigned were Hudsons Nos. 3460-3465. When No. 3461 was delivered by Baldwin in October 1937, it was the first new steam locomotive to arrive on the property since 1930. No. 3460, the last of the six Hudsons to be

Steam power and stainless steel were an intriguing combination in the early years of the streamlined *Chief*, a train that kept its all-Pullman status from its inauguration in 1926 until 1954. Though a streamliner from 1938 onward, the train often carried heavyweight head-end cars. Top, on November 10, 1941, the *Chief* — seen here at Wilbern, Illinois — has a stainless-steel RPO but heavyweight baggage. Bottom left, with a Northern on the point and an all-heavyweight head-end consist, the *Chief* climbs Cajon Pass in California. Green flags indicate a second section following. Bottom right, with "Blue Goose" Hudson and lightweight baggage-lounge, this is an all-streamlined *Chief*. GORDON C. BASSETT COLLECTION, TOP; SANTA FE RAILWAY, BOTTOM

Drifting smoke betrays steam on the head end of this *Chief* on Cajon Pass, trailing a *Betahtakin* -class 4-drawing-room 1-double-bedroom lounge-observation. SANTA FE RAILWAY

completed, was the one-of-a-kind streamlined "Blue Goose." Much akin to ten New Haven "Shoreliners" also delivered in 1937 by Baldwin, it was Santa Fe's only fully streamlined steamer. Its shrouding was painted medium and light blue trimmed with stainless steel, and its running gear was blue-gray. Driver tires and other wheel rims were painted aluminum. Less glamorous but handsome and efficient were Baldwin's even newer Northerns—Nos. 3765-3775—that generally hauled the *Chief* west of La Junta.

In fact, the *Chief* was inferior to the *Super* only in the matter of speed. Were there any question about the parity of equipment between the two trains, the circumstances of the entry into service of the second *Super Chief* consist would remove it.

On February 22, 1938, the *Super* received a second set of equipment, enabling it to go semiweekly, and was joined by an all-coach running mate, the pocket streamliner *El Capitan,* also operating twice a week on a 39-hour 45-minute schedule. At this time, minor modifications were made in the consist of the initial streamlined *Super Chief.* Baggage car No. 3430 was withdrawn and replaced by Budd-built baggage-dormitory-buffet lounge *San Clemente,* and Pullman-Standard's *Tuba,* a 17-roomette car from the *Chief* pool, was added.

In keeping with Santa Fe's new policy, Pullman-Standard was to supply the six sleepers for the second *Super* consist — *Chimayo, Talwiwi, Tchirege, Tsankawi, Tyuonyi,* and observation *Puye*—but when February rolled around they were nowhere near ready. The solution was to pull equivalent cars—*Chinle, Wupatki, Klethla, Polacca, Yampai,* and *Chaistla*—from the sixth, standby *Chief* consist. That this could be done without diminution of quality was clear evidence that the *Chief* gave up little but speed to its slightly more illustrious running mate. When the intended sleepers finally arrived from P-S in June and July, they entered the consist. Budd's only contributions to this second streamlined *Super Chief* were baggage-dormitory-buffet lounge *San Acacia,* dormitory-barber shop-club lounge *Agathla,* and diner *Awatobi*.

But the fleet of coach streamliners that would be inaugurated in 1938 beginning with *El Capitan* re-

A pair of views of No. 20, the eastbound *Chief,* on Cajon Pass with sister Northerns. Above, No. 3767 works near Alray, California, on October 11, 1939. Below, No. 3768 is rolling at Summit on November 2, 1941. RICHARD H. KINDIG

Right, the routine drama of picking up mail on the fly as performed by the eastbound *Chief* at Monrovia, California: the clerk aboard the heavyweight RPO car has used the extendable arm by the car door to snare the sack strung up on the standard; a sack the clerk has off-loaded kicks dust in the foreground. Below, smoke towers over double-shotted steam working hard at Lamy, New Mexico, on March 31, 1946. Facing page: This classic view of passengers boarding the glamorous *Super Chief* in dowdy Dearborn Station, Chicago, illustrates the Santa Fe's unusual but welcome practice of adorning bumping posts with illuminated carbon copies of the streamliners' drumheads. This custom continued long after the observation cars and then the trains' drumheads themselves disappeared. SANTA FE RAILWAY, RIGHT AND FACING PAGE; STAN KISTLER, BELOW

mained the sole province of Budd. The five-car consists that inaugurated the *El Cap* comprised a baggage-dormitory-32-seat chair car with conductor's desk and newsstand, two 52-seat chair cars, a lunch-counter diner (with counter seating for fourteen and a more formal section with six tables for four), and a 50-seat chair-observation. All the chair-car seats pivoted to face the window for better viewing or all the way around so passengers could converse with their neighbors.

The decor throughout the train was dominated by soft, warm tones and varied from car to car to avoid monotony. Contrasting shades were used subtly: old rose with red, buff with tans, olive with gray-greens, all highlighted by stainless steel and chrome trim. The side walls of all the cars were finished in Flexwood Veneer.

Specific Electro-Motive E1's were assigned as power for each of these early streamliners: Nos. 3 and 3A to the second *Super* (with Nos. 4 and 4A as backup) and Nos. 5 and 6 to the two short *El Capitan* consists.

An early brochure touted the pocket streamliner this way: "Someone has called *El Capitan* 'A Fascinating Experiment in Practical Democracy.' That is because *El Capitan* is America's first and only deluxe all-chair-car transcontinental train; because, though *El Capitan* is beautiful and ultramodern, and as swift as the finest of the deluxe streamliners, it was designed and built entirely for the joy and convenience of the economically minded. . . ." The extra fare was a modest $4 maximum, compared to $10 for the *Super Chief*. It *was* an unprecedented concept—a chair-car-only train on the same fast schedule as the all-Pullman flagship.

The idea had been clearly articulated as far back as February 18, 1936—even before the inauguration of the heavyweight *Super Chief*—by C. T. Ripley, Santa Fe's chief mechanical engineer, in a letter to John Purcell, assistant to the vice-president. Having just ridden to the west coast aboard the Budd-built experimental chair car No. 3070, Ripley had these observations on coach service: "I think where we are making a serious mistake in the present day trains, is attempting to combine this type of travel with Pullman service. We arouse the resentment of coach passengers by shutting them out of certain facilities on the train. They also are not interested in high priced dinner service, and also object very much to the excessive charge involved when they wish to get a berth for the night. I am of the opinion that if a regular coach train were run, in which the equipment were especially designed for the service, a large amount of new business could be secured. . . . I would call this train the 'Economy Chief.' '' (Other names later suggested and rejected included Little Chief, Conquistador, Nonpareil, Paragon, Paramount, Champion, Vencedor, and Vogue—for the most part semantic reactions to Union Pacific's directly competing *Challenger,* inaugurated in 1935.)

Ripley proposed an eight-car train, which would have included an RPO, a club-coach, two chair cars just like prototype 3070, a ladies' coach (with no men's lounge and thus more coach seats), a coffee shop car, a special sleeper with 32 berths (not reservable in advance, for ''older people or sick people, who wish to go to bed,'' costing $1 for an upper and $2 for a lower), and a parlor observation with the parlor seats renting for $1 a day or 50¢ a half-day. ''This train would have a total capacity of about 275 passengers and should be operated for about 75¢ per mile, including overhead charges,'' according to Ripley, who was certainly on to something, though the sleeper and parlor options were not part of the shorter train actually built later.

But Ripley's general idea clearly had merit, and it wouldn't take long for the little trains to grow from their original five cars, filling out with the coaches delivered for that other economy train, the *Scout*. In the summer of 1939 *El Cap* added three coaches and a second diner. By 1940 the *El Capitan* consist would typically be ten or more cars long and include a chair-car lounge, ''with its modern cocktail bar, roomy davenports, lounging chairs, and radio—an especially popular place for jolly parties or for individual relaxation,'' according to Santa Fe's publicity pamphlet. This longer consist required two diesel units. By the mid-forties the train would swell to a dozen cars, including two lunch-counter diners and a full lounge.

But it was a diminutive five-car consist that went on pre-inaugural display and tour in 1938. On February 12 and 13 *El Capitan* was on exhibition in Chicago's Dearborn Station, along with the second *Super Chief*

consist, which like *El Cap* was about to enter service, and a lightweight *Chief* powered by streamlined Hudson 3460. More than 30,000 visitors passed through the trains, and thousands more were turned away. The next day, at 7:00 p.m., one *El Cap* and the new *Super* left on a trial run to Los Angeles—coupled together behind their combined three E1's in a move that foreshadowed the routine operating practice of the trains' later years, when they ran as a single, combined consist except at times of peak demand.

Exhibition stops were made at Kansas City and Albuquerque, on the way to a 7:00 a.m. arrival in Los Angeles on February 17. The next day *El Capitan* made a preview run to the Grand Canyon for the press and company officials, returning two days later to Los Angeles, where the consist joined the *Chief* and *Super Chief,* already on display there. Then, on February 22, *El Capitan* and the *Super Chief* began twice-weekly service, with consists of both trains converging from both endpoints. Chicago departures were on Tuesdays and Saturdays (5:45 p.m. for *El Cap* and 7:15 p.m. for the *Super*) and Los Angeles departures Tuesdays and Fridays (1:30 p.m. and 8 p.m.).

One of the special features of *El Capitan* was the courier-nurses, a service that had actually been inaugurated in June of 1937, aboard the *Scout*. After expansion the next year to serve *El Capitan,* the corps numbered seventeen young women, aged twenty-four

This booklet, issued in 1938, when the *Chief* was streamlined and the *Super Chief* made twice-weekly, touted both trains together, showing the parity of equipment between them.
PETER TILP COLLECTION

THE *Super Chief* and *Chief* are frankly designed for those who seek the utmost in swift, luxurious travel to and from California.

They are the flag-bearers of that great fleet of sixteen gleaming streamliners with which Santa Fe has brought new delight in travel to those who journey between Chicago and California and in the Southwest.

The *Super Chief* and *Chief* are extra fare, air-conditioned trains. They are alike in their superb Fred Harvey cuisine, and in the type, modernity and beauty of their equipment.

Beyond this, each has its own special features that we hope will appeal as strongly to you as they have to the long roll of discriminating travelers in whose esteem the *Super Chief* and the *Chief* already hold a high and friendly place.

T. B. Gallaher

Passenger Traffic Manager, Santa Fe System Lines, Chicago, Illinois.

FORWARD LOUNGE

Inasmuch as the *Super Chief* and *Chief* are both superb extra fare streamliners, for first-class travel only, their accommodations and services are almost identical. Hence these natural color photographs and brief descriptions apply equally to either train • Pictured here is the forward lounge, one of the three cars providing cheery, roomy, and convenient lounge facilities, regardless of the location of one's accommodations.

SECTIONS

The section is a combination of an upper and lower berth by night, and of two comfortable facing window seats by day. Upper or lower berths may be purchased separately, of course. When a section is reserved for one person, however, the upper berth is not made down, giving additional space and privacy at night, and use of both window seats during the day. Section accommodations on the *Super Chief* and *Chief* are the latest and most attractive type.

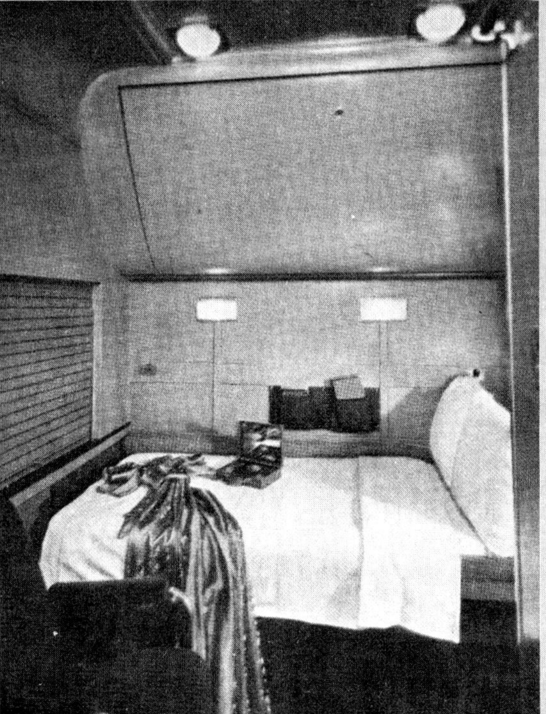

DRAWING ROOMS

Spacious comfort keynotes the new drawing rooms on the *Super Chief* and *Chief*, due to the complete rearrangement of facilities, combined with tasteful decoration, and modern lighting and appointments. By day there are two lounge chairs and a long sofa. At night the sofa becomes a bed; another bed materializes from the wall, and an upper berth is available, if desired. There is a complete toilet annex, a large wardrobe, ample storage for luggage, a shoe box, and individual regulation of lighting and ventilation.

FRED HARVEY DINING CAR SERVICE

For more than half a century discriminating travelers have recognized Fred Harvey dining car service on the Santa Fe as outstanding in the transportation world. This famous service reaches its finest expression in the beautiful diners of the *Super Chief* and *Chief*, with their carefully chosen personnel, their gleaming silver and glassware, snowy napery and especially designed china. Breakfast and luncheon are served a la carte; dinner, both a la carte and table d'hote.

OBSERVATION LOUNGE

The observation lounge, in the rear room car on the *Super Chief* and *Chief*, supplements the forward lounge, and the cocktail lounge near the center of the train, in providing that generous extra space for relaxation that is so welcome a feature of fine train travel. In the observation lounge you will find another writing desk, with distinctive train stationery, and a wide selection of current periodicals, while broad windows permit sweeping views of the passing scenery.

Club Lounge Car

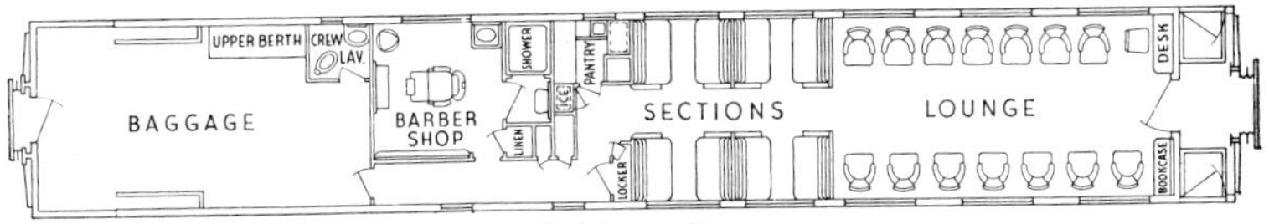

Club Baggage Car

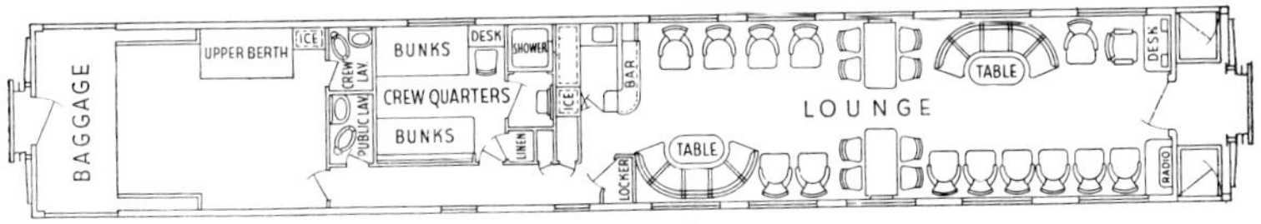

Club Baggage Car

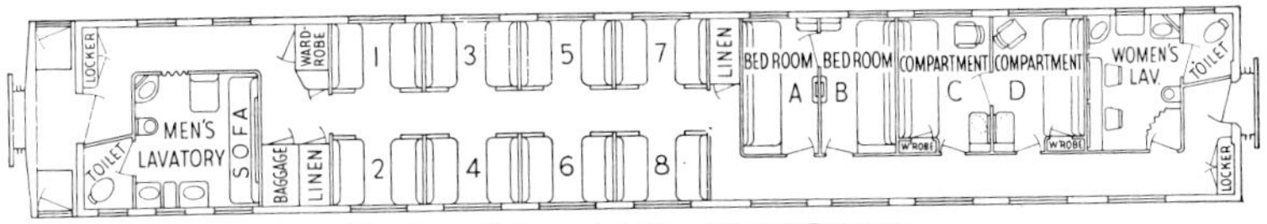

8 Sections — 2 Compartments — 2 Double Bedrooms

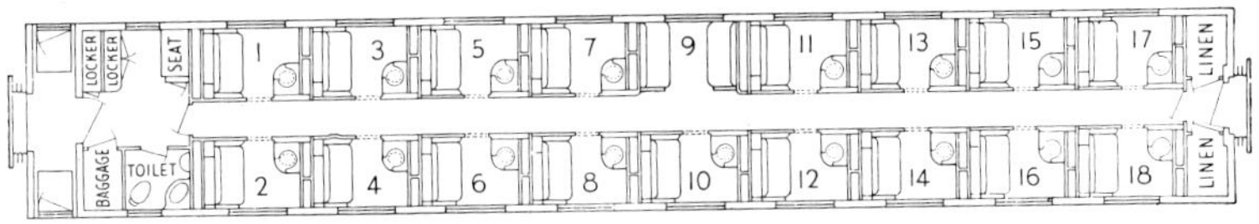

17 Roomettes

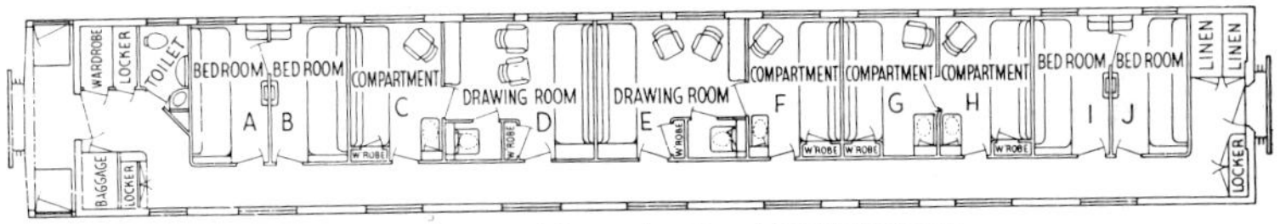

2 Drawing Rooms — 4 Compartments — 4 Double Bedrooms

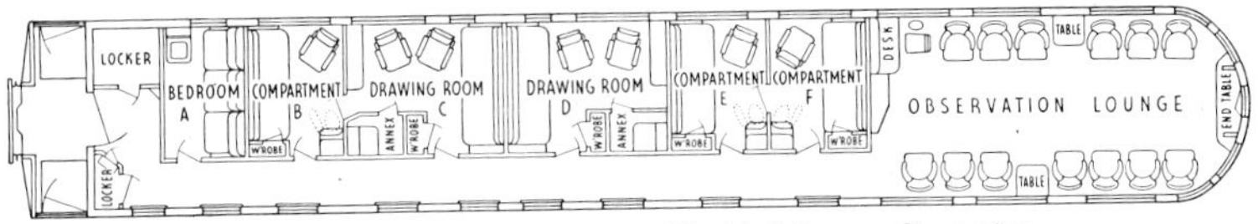

3 Compartments — 2 Drawing Rooms — 1 Double Bedroom — Observation

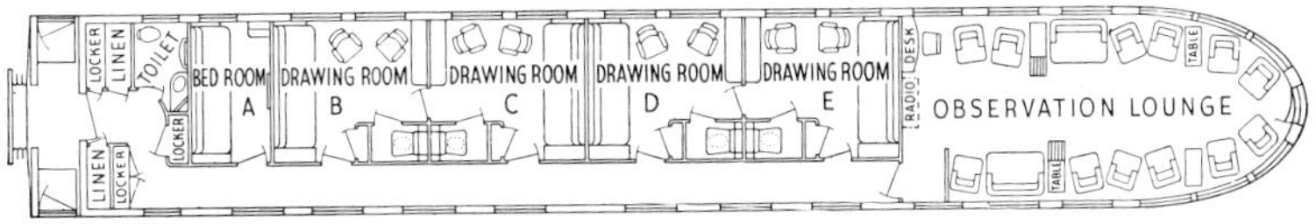

4 Drawing Rooms — 1 Double Bedroom — Observation

Right, *El Capitan*'s Budd-built chair-observation. Below, this view in Los Angeles — at Santa Fe's old La Grande Station, replaced in July 1939 by Los Angeles Union Passenger Terminal — is of *El Cap*'s early days, with the original five-car consist. Facing page, before its new transcontinental equipment went into service in February 1938, Santa Fe set it out in its Chicago Coach Yard for a photo session. The observation lineup — Budd's flatter-faced *El Cap* cars flanking Pullman-Standard's more gradually tapered *Super Chief* and *Chief* sleepers — shows clearly this stylistic difference between the two builders. In the locomotive lineup, E1 No. 2, power for the first streamlined *Super,* is at the far left, next to sister E1's Nos. 3, 5, and 6, and the "Blue Goose." SANTA FE RAILWAY

to twenty-nine. Their duties were "to attend mothers with babies and children, to watch over youngsters traveling alone, to administer to invalids and the aged, and to assist all others who may require their friendly service." The women hired had to be graduate registered nurses (preferably college-educated), unmarried, about 5' 6" tall, weighing 125-135 pounds, of "direct and courteous manner," with a "pleasing personality" and "good appearance."

Once hired for this rigorous job—one Chicago-Los Angeles round trip each ten days, on duty from 6:30 a.m. to 10:00 p.m. and on call at night—the women tried out the "Indian Detours" for tourists that Fred Harvey and Santa Fe had long promoted and generally became knowledgeable about the Southwest so they could explain the region's sights to the passengers. Though all this may seem onerous, the positions were much in demand and there was little turnover; only twenty women left in the first five years, fifteen of those to be married.

The service proved a great success, as the nurses entertained children with bedtime stories and other "wholesome recreation" and cared for babies while their mothers ate in the diner. In 1941, for instance, they oversaw 1,175 unaccompanied children, prepared 2,575 baby formulas, and cared for approximately 18,000 children under twelve. Aboard *El Cap,* as Ripley had suggested years earlier in his letter, the fourth car was set aside exclusively for women and children, and the washroom in that car especially equipped as headquarters for the courier-nurse.

Once the transcontinental streamliners were rolling, Santa Fe turned its attention to the short hauls. The first was the *San Diegan,* which began regular service on March 27, 1938—a single consist making two round trips daily over the 126-mile route between Los Angeles and San Diego. Behind Electro-Motive E1 No. 7 was baggage-mail-express No. 3400 (bumped from the original *Super Chief* consist), two 60-seat chair cars (from the *Scout* order), a lunch-counter-tavern diner, and a parlor-observation lounge, all built by Budd. More coaches were added almost immediately; in time this consist, like *El Capitan*'s, would swell considerably with extra cars, more than doubling capacity. And on June 8, 1941, a second *San Diegan*

El Capitan
Chief
Chief
El Capitan

SANTA FE
SANTA FE
3460
3460
Santa Fe
SANTA FE
SANTA FE

3775

Facing page: Waiting west of Ayer on a nippy Colorado morning — February 22, 1939 — photographer Otto Perry was well placed to record Santa Fe's triology of transcontinental streamliners. Just after eight o'clock the first rolled into view, headed west: No. 21, the little five-car *El Cap*, clipping along at 75 miles-per-hour (top). Almost on its heels was No. 19, the *Chief*, behind Northern 3775 and running hardly slower, showing that steam was no slouch (bottom left). Ninety minutes later followed the flagship — the *Super Chief* — also scorching gravel. Right, E1 No. 3 — the power for the second streamlined *Super Chief* consist — is hoisted off its trucks for maintenance. OTTO C. PERRY, DENVER PUBLIC LIBRARY, WESTERN HISTORY COLLECTION, FACING PAGE; SANTA FE RAILWAY, ROBERT J. WAYNER COLLECTION, RIGHT

streamliner would enter service, allowing four daily round trips, plus two more protected by a heavyweight consist.

Possibly because the *Chief, Super Chief,* and *El Capitan* had been exhibiting in the area just a month before, leaving the usual dignitaries already sated with stainless steel, the *San Diegan*'s inaugural ceremonies had an unusual twist: the guests of honor were high-school students. On March 19 the San Diego Chamber of Commerce invited a group of Los Angeles-area students to come to San Diego for the day aboard a preview run of the train. On March 21 the Los Angeles Chamber returned the favor. There were gardenias for the girls and carnation boutonnieres for the boys, and souvenir pencils for all. According to the *The Santa Fe Magazine,* "it was an inspiring sight to see these fine young people walk with that fresh stride of youth to the gleaming streamliner—the *San Diegan*—eyes sparkling, lips bubbling with youth's ever-ready quips."

The following month, on April 17, another new daylight streamliner was inaugurated—the *Kansas Cityan-Chicagoan* pair in daily service between Chicago and Wichita, Kansas, via Kansas City. The consists for these trains were similar to the *San Diegan*'s, though more luxurious; they were, in fact, the most deluxe of the daytime streamliners, appropriately in that their journey was the longest. Again, they were entirely Budd-built. Instead of the *San Diegan*'s lunch-counter diner, the new trains had full 48-seat diners; and one of their four coaches was a handsome club lounge-chair car. (The other chair cars were 52-seaters, not 60-seaters, more comfortable for long-distance travel.) These cars were all sandwiched between a baggage-mail-express and parlor-observation-lounge, sisters of the *San Diegan*'s cars.

Westbound the train was No. 11, the *Kansas Cityan,* and eastbound No. 12, the *Chicagoan*. In either direction, the running time was 11 hours and 45 minutes (nipping in under the 12-hour mark by a margin reminiscent of the *Super* and *El Cap*'s 39 hours and 45 minutes) for the 663 miles between Chicago and Wichita.

Naturally, before entering service the new trains were opened to the public—at Wichita and Topeka, Kansas, where there were also the obligatory ceremonial luncheons. For these exhibitions and for the initial months of operation, power was Electro-Motive's E1's Nos. 8 and 9 (the last built of these handsome, sleek locomotives with recessed headlights and generally impeccable streamlining). In June, however, these two units headed west to power the new *Golden Gate* trains, which would soon be inaugurated.

Replacing them were two strange beasts: "Amos 'n' Andy," rebuilt at Topeka Shops into something vaguely streamlined, with 1A becoming No. 1 and 1B becoming No. 10. These rebuilds looked a bit like E1's that had run into a brick wall, their blunt snouts rounded but squashed with their cabs pushed high above them.

The *San Diegan*'s lounge interior (top) and Budd-built obs, seen as the train runs along Pacific Ocean beaches (bottom). Just ahead of the observation is No. 1100, the experimental 56-seat "Pendulum" chair car built for Santa Fe by Pacific Railway Equipment Company in 1941; the car, not successful enough to be duplicated, tested in the Los Angeles area. SANTA FE RAILWAY

(Two years later 10 was rebuilt to a booster.) Perhaps their assignment to these trains which passed daily hrough Topeka was designed to keep them near the shops where they were reborn.

The *Golden Gate,* which on July 1, 1938, became the next entry in Santa Fe's streamliner sweepstakes, was an intermodal venture: San Francisco-Oakland by bus, Oakland-Bakersfield by train, Bakersfield-Los Angeles by bus. All vehicles, rail or road, were streamlined and air-conditioned. The five-car trains, headed by E1's Nos. 8 and 9, each carried a baggage-36-seat chair car, two 52-seat chair cars, a 60-seat chair car-observation, and a lunch-counter tavern like the *San Diegan*'s. As with all the Santa Fe streamliners, considerable care was taken in choosing the name "Golden Gate." Also in the running were Wawana, El Capitan, Yosemite, Bret Harte, Mark Twain, San Pablo, Fort Tejon, Bay City, The Eagle, and The Hawk—the latter two favored for a time by Roger Birdseye.

Prior to inauguration the two consists were on display, most notably on the State Belt tracks along San Francisco's Embarcadero for two days but also briefly at nearly two dozen on-line communities, most of them tiny. "Good-will tours," as Santa Fe always called them, were made on June 28 to Fresno by the San Francisco Chamber of Commerce and on June 29 to San Francisco by the Bakersfield Chamber. Two days later the trains went into regular service, offering twice-daily round trips from San Francisco to Los Angeles as Nos. 60, 61, 62, and 63, the entire combined bus-and-train journey taking 9 hours and 20 minutes.

An interesting running mate joined the *Golden Gate* on its route through the San Joaquin Valley just under a year later, on June 11, 1939: the steam-hauled, six-car *Valley Flyer*. This colorful train of refurbished, air-conditioned heavyweights—a baggage-club, a refreshment car, three coaches, and a diner—was decked out in bright red, yellow, and silver and powered by one of two semi-streamlined Pacifics painted to match: Nos. 1369 or 1376. The *Flyer* made a daily round trip between Oakland and Bakersfield, with bus connections to San Francisco and Los Angeles. (Two through trains from Chicago, the *Navajo* and the *Grand Canyon*

Above, the *Chicagoan* drumhead on the train's Budd-built parlor-observation lounge. After the *Tulsan*'s inauguration on December 10, 1939, the *Chicagoan/Kansas Cityan* parlor-observations ran through between Kansas City and Tulsa on that train. Top right, the *Chicagoan/Kansas Cityan* in early years most often was powered by Nos. 1 or 10 — rebuilds from the original heavyweight *Super Chief* diesels 1A and 1B. Here, No. 10 leads the *Chicagoan* out of Emporia, Kansas, on March 4, 1939, with a consist as originally delivered: baggage-mail-express, four coaches (one of them with lounge facilities), and parlor-observation lounge. Bottom right, on May 11, 1940, E6 No. 12 powers the *Kansas Cityan* through Chillicothe, Illinois. Head-end cars here are a full RPO and a baggage-dormitory-coach. SANTA FE RAILWAY, ABOVE; OTTO C. PERRY, DENVER PUBLIC LIBRARY, AMERICAN HISTORY COLLECTION, TOP RIGHT; GORDON C. BASSETT COLLECTION, BOTTOM RIGHT

Right, less than four months into its career — on August 2, 1938 — the *Kansas Cityan* rolls west through Chillicothe behind No. 1, which originally had been half of "Amos 'n' Andy." Below, again at Chillicothe, No. 10 — the other of those boxy diesels which originally powered the heavyweight *Super* — now teams with E1A No. 4 (purchased as back-up power for the streamlined *Super Chief*) to haul the *Chief* on January 30, 1941. GORDON C. BASSETT COLLECTION

Limited, also had bus connections and could be used for L.A.-San Francisco travel.) The *Valley Flyer* was short-lived, operating just for the term of the Golden Gate International Exposition in San Francisco; later the consist ran on the *San Diegan* route.

The *Golden Gate*'s July 1 inaugural concluded a feverish half-year's activity which saw fourteen new streamlined consists enter service—making the Santa Fe the largest operator of streamliners in the country. Just one train remained to complete the railroad's first surge of streamlining, and that was the *Tulsan*, something of an afterclap, entering service almost eighteen months later, on December 10, 1939. In addition to the new train itself—a Kansas City-Tulsa round trip carrying numbers 211 and 212—this inaugural involved the restructuring and extension of the railroad's Oklahoma passenger service in general.

The *Tulsan* made a direct connection at Kansas City with Nos. 11 and 12, the *Kansas Cityan* and *Chicagoan;* in fact, the parlor-observation from those trains was interchanged with the *Tulsan* there, rather than operating west to and from Wichita as it had previously. The new Tulsa-Chicago service took just 12 hours and 40 minutes for the 707 miles—an improvement of six hours over the previous time.

Also on December 10, Nos. 11 and 12 were extended from Wichita to Oklahoma City, a fifteen-hour journey from Chicago. One coach from that train ran on to Fort Worth and Dallas in Nos. 15 and 16, along with a through sleeper—a 14-section lightweight—from Kansas City. And the existing overnight sleeping-car service between Tulsa and Chicago was put on a faster and more convenient schedule.

The name *Tulsan* was chosen in a contest, begun the first day the train was placed on exhibition and continuing through one month of regular service. (Initial publicity called the train simply "new streamliner.") Entry blanks were available to all who visited the train on display or traveled aboard it during the contest period. Contestants were asked to suggest names and explain their choices in brief statements. The prize was $250. On February 13 the winner was announced: Mrs. Corrine Terry, a bookkeeper from Tulsa. Of 4506 entries, 127 had suggested "Tulsan," but the judges found Mrs. Terry's statement the most worthy: "Being the first three letters of Tulsa and Santa Fe combined, and consistent with two other important names of your service, the *Kansas Cityan* going to Kansas City and the *Chicagoan* going to Chicago, this seems most appropriate for a train of such beauty, comfort, and speed."

Beauty, comfort, and speed: that described the *Super Chief, Chief, El Capitan, San Diegan, Golden Gate, Chicagoan, Kansas Cityan,* and *Tulsan,* seventeen consists of nearly unbroken stainless steel. The first years of the forties saw Santa Fe adding motive power—seven Electro-Motive E6's (four A units and three B's) and an A/B set of Alco DL109's—as well as additional lightweight cars to fill out all the coach streamliner consists in response to increasing demand for space.

During those years a total of fifty-six assorted baggage, baggage-mail, baggage-dormitory, baggage-chair, railway post office, dining, lunch-counter, and chair cars were delivered to swell the streamliners and to mix in otherwise heavyweight consists of secondary trains. Of the total number, fifty-two came from Budd, three from Pullman-Standard, and one from Pacific Railway Equipment Company—an interesting, experimental and never-duplicated 56-seat Pendulum Chair Car, No. 1100, delivered in November of 1941.

In addition, in June of 1942 Pullman-Standard delivered twenty-six *Valley*-series 6-section 6-roomette 4-double-bedroom sleepers—*Antelope Valley* to *Whitewater Valley*—for *California Limited* service, operating on the Chicago-Los Angeles, Chicago-Oakland, Kansas City-Los Angeles, and Denver-Los Angeles lines. These two-tone-gray *Valley* cars also showed up on the *Chief*. Further, three cars from this order went into Chicago-Kansas City-Tulsa service.

In roughly five years, Santa Fe had put an extraodinary lightweight fleet in place, and none too soon. Every inch of its substantial capacity would be taxed by World War II.

Top, Budd's 60-seat chair car-observations built for the *Golden Gate* were external look-alikes to the *El Cap, San Diegan,* and *Chicagoan/Kansas Cityan* obs cars — but identical in configuration to none of them. Bottom, the *Valley Flyer* was only briefly a running mate for the *Golden Gate.* SANTA FE RAILWAY, TOP AND BOTTOM LEFT; W. C. WHITTAKER, ROBERT J. WAYNER COLLECTION, BOTTOM RIGHT

PASADENA
3
1581
SANTA FE

5

Postwar Improvements

On its new postwar every-other-day schedule, the westbound *El Capitan* arrives at Pasadena, California, on July 11, 1946, behind FT's newly rebuilt for passenger service. No. 158 was one of ten A-B-B-A FT sets originally delivered as freighters but modified to haul streamliners and other varnish. STAN KISTLER

World War II did indeed stretch Santa Fe's passenger-carrying capacity to the breaking point, figuratively running the wheels off the huge collection of coaches, diners, and Pullmans that the railroad had assumed in the previous five years. Passenger loadings on both the *Chief* and the *Super Chief* rocketed from an average of eighty or ninety to 150, and even more dramatic growth occurred on the less illustrious trains. For the first half of 1942, the passenger-mile total was 1,075,941,672 compared to 571,220,535 the previous year—an 88 percent increase. Santa Fe had the largest fleet of streamliners in the world, and this resource was tested to the fullest.

Another simple yardstick to measure this traffic growth was the business in the Fred Harvey diners. The dining-car department—which comprised eighty cars and 106 crews—in 1943 was doing about 200 percent more business than it had in peacetime. On some trains, notably Nos. 1 and 2, the *Scout,* as many as 350 passengers would appear for a single meal—which, in the standard Santa Fe 36-seat diner, meant ten sittings.

Obviously quantity, not quality, was the measure of success in these troubled years. Not until the war ended in 1945 could Santa Fe management again emphasize the elegant and stylish service that had been the hallmark of its streamliners in prewar years. Santa Fe laid plans immediately for substantial re-equippings, ordering 156 new lightweight cars, including fifty-one all-room sleepers.

But Santa Fe was not alone during those first postwar years in its desire to make up for lost time in the passenger-train competition; car and locomotive builders were flooded with orders from railroads across the land, orders which when fulfilled would create the last great passenger-train boom in the United States. Thus it was not until 1947 that new cars began to arrive at Santa Fe, allowing the most important postwar improvements to occur in early 1948: the re-equipping of the *Super Chief* and *El Capitan,* which at the same time became daily trains; and the inauguration of the Chicago-Galveston *Texas Chief.*

A substantial array of new diesels—Alco PA's, Electro-Motive FT's and F3's, and one A-B-A set of Fairbanks-Morse "Erie-builts"—began to arrive as early as 1945, adding muscle to the passenger power pool. Eventually there would be a dozen A-B-A sets of Alco's graceful 2000-horsepower PA's, delivered between October 1946 and December 1948. Each lash-up totalled 6000-horsepower, the same as the set of "Erie-builts" and each of the A-B-B-A lash-ups of F3's—twenty-four of which were delivered between September 1946 and January 1949, a total of ninety-six units.

The first postwar passenger diesels acquired were Electro-Motive FT's. Santa Fe had in freight service a

Above, on March 28, 1946, there are still traces of snow on the hillside. Triple-shotted steamers — 2-10-2's No. 3806 and 1705 and 4-8-4 No. 3785 — are down to 25 miles per hour as they tug a long *Chief* (fifteen cars, including four heavyweights on the head end) up Raton Pass, near Lynn, Colorado. No. 3806's green flags suggest that there's more to come. RICHARD H. KINDIG, PETER TILP COLLECTION. Facing page: top, seen here on the *Chief* at Pasadena in July 1945, FT No. 167 had been delivered five months earlier in the standard blue and yellow freight scheme but classed dual-service, as it was geared for passenger-hauling and contained steam generators in the two B-units. No. 167's success led to a postwar order for F3 passenger units — as well as the conversion of ten FT A-B-B-A sets for passenger service (Nos. 158 through 166, and 168). No. 167 received the "warbonnet" passenger scheme in mid-1946, and its converted sisters were repainted as well. All the FT's returned to freight service in late 1949. Bottom left, one of those converted FT's, No. 161, grinds upgrade at 20 miles-an-hour near Wootton, Colorado, on the morning of May 18, 1946, with the westbound *Chief*. Bottom right, standard railroading remained very much a part of the Santa Fe, even after the once-steam-hauled streamlined *Chief* had been dieselized. Here second No. 3, the all-heavyweight, steam-powered *California Limited,* clouds the sky west of Romero, New Mexico, in October of 1947. STAN KISTLER, TOP; RICHARD H. KINDIG, BOTTOM

huge fleet of these pioneering units, purchased from December 1940 through August 1945. These 1350-horsepower diesels also arrived in four-unit sets, each generating 5400 horsepower. (The first FT sets were configured A-B-B-B, due to initial insistence by the Brotherhood of Locomotive Engineers that two cabs equalled two locomotives, which required two crews.) A single set of FT's—No. 167—geared for 95-mile-per-hour passenger service was delivered in February 1945, painted in blue freight livery. The two booster units had steam boilers and water tanks.

Tests with these units proved successful; so, between April and August 1945, Santa Fe converted ten freight FT A-B-B-A sets to passenger service. These forty units were regeared for one-hundred-mile-per-hour running and given second headlights, tightlock couplers, and the flashy passenger paint scheme. Boilers and extra water tanks—actually just what otherwise would have been fuel tanks—were added to the booster units.

Train 20, the eastbound *Chief,* is thirteen cars long on September 22, 1947, seen here at Cajon, California. No. 158 is the lowest-numbered of the eleven passenger FT sets. ROBERT F. COLLINS

Though the F-unit fleet initiated by the FT's and F3's proved highly successful and ultimately set the pattern for future Santa Fe motive-power purchases, the introduction of the Alco PA's in 1946 provided the most excitement and panache at the time. These long, angular, six-wheel-trucked locomotives were inherently glamorous; and No. 51, the first of Santa Fe's fleet of twelve sets, was also the 75,000th locomotive built by American Locomotive Company. Thus its debut attracted even more attention—particularly since that debut was at the Waldorf-Astoria Hotel in New York City.

The rangy A-B-A diesel set was displayed under the Waldorf, two floors below street level on a siding that was an adjunct of Grand Central Terminal. This siding in the dark bowels of the earth had been intended to accommodate the private cars of rich and powerful Waldorf denizens. For this celebratory occasion it had been transformed—by the artifice of a stage designer—into a desert scene typical of the Southwest that would be home for Santa Fe's PA's. Creative lighting, along with a synthetic grass carpet and desert trees, cacti, and other plants did the trick.

The PA's—along with a full-sized model of the *Sandusky,* the first locomotive built by Alco, in 1837—were exhibited September 22-24, and there was a succession of luncheons, suppers, and receptions at the Waldorf for the press, traffic managers and shippers, business executives, financiers, and Alco and Santa Fe employees and their families. Indians of the Zuni, Apache, and Jemez tribes came from the Southwest to perform traditional dances; on display were a series of railroad paintings by Howard Fogg, then a young artist with a growing reputation.

Radio commentator Lowell Thomas gave a broadcast from No. 51's cab. The festivities culminated in a dinner in the grand ballroom of the Waldorf, filled to overflowing with 1,200 bankers, industrialists, and railroad executives. The host was R. B. McColl, president of Alco, and the honoree was Santa Fe's President Fred G. Gurley, reflecting the dual aegis of the PA's debut.

All this new motive power would eventually make many things possible, including a daily *Super Chief* and a daily *El Capitan* in February 1948. The first step in that direction came in September 1946 when these trains, now powered most often by FT's, were increased from twice weekly to every other day, with the two trains operating on alternate days. By the summer of 1947, the long-steam-powered *Chief* had finally been dieselized, which made possible a June 8

Left, one-of-a-kind, Pullman-pool, round-end, all-aluminum sleeper-observation lounge *George M. Pullman* — built in 1933 for exhibition at the Century of Progress Exposition in Chicago and regarded as a transitional car between the heavyweight and lightweight eras — carried the markers and *Chief* drumhead on June 21, 1946, near Summit, California. Bottom, when postwar diesel proliferation brought numerous Alco PA's to the passenger roster, the only diesel kin they found was a single 2000-horsepower DL-109/110 set — Cab unit DL-109 No. 50 and booster DL-110 No. 50A — delivered by Alco in 1941. Santa Fe was one of just seven railroads to own DL-109/110's, which were styled by Otto Kuhler. RICHARD H. KINDIG, PETER TILP COLLECTION, LEFT; SANTA FE RAILWAY, BOTTOM

Left: FT-powered *Chief* in vastly different settings: curving through the Colorado hills near Wootton in 1946, trailing observation *Denehotso* (top); and awaiting departure from Dearborn Station, with Chicago's gritty skyline in the background (bottom). RICHARD H. KINDIG, PETER TILP COLLECTION, TOP; SANTA FE, BOTTOM. Facing page: As rare as ATSF's single Alco DL-109/110 was its lone Fairbanks-Morse "Erie-built" trio — cab-booster-cab Nos. 50-50A-50B. This lanky locomotive is seen in the engine terminal at Los Angeles (top left); at San Diego in September 1953, running as a train normally protected by a Budd Car (top right); and rounding a curve between Summit and Cajon, California, with the first section of the jack-of-all- trades *Grand Canyon* on April 4, 1954. SANTA FE RAILWAY, TOP LEFT; FRED MATTHEWS, TOP RIGHT; STAN KISTLER, BOTTOM

schedule reduction from 48 hours to 46 hours eastbound and 46 hours 30 minutes westbound.

Also on that date the *Grand Canyon* was dieselized (allowing the timings for this workhorse to be cut to 48 hours 45 minutes Chicago-Los Angeles and 55 hours 15 minutes Chicago-San Francisco) and streamlined with prewar lightweights as new cars destined to inaugurate the *Texas Chief* and allow the *Super Chief* and *El Cap* to go daily began to arrive. Another innovation in the consist was a lightweight sleeper for Fort Worth carried from Los Angeles. Also in the summer of 1947, the Santa Fe's first postwar sleepers arrived—a dozen *Indian*-series 24-duplex-roomette cars from Pullman-Standard, the only such fleet ever to operate in the United States. These cars entered service on the *Grand Canyon* and the *Ranger*.

Some service enhancements did not require new equipment, and these were made even sooner. On March 1, 1947, courier-nurses had been returned to the *El Capitan* and *Scout* after a wartime lapse of nearly five years. A new staff of twenty-six registered nurses was recruited, largely World War II veterans of the Army or Navy nursing corps. This service, begun back in 1937, had proven very popular—particularly among passengers with small children, the ill or convalescing, or the aged, those who received the most attention from the nurses.

Even earlier had come the inauguration of coast-to-coast through sleeper service, an improvement planned before the war but not accomplished until after its conclusion. On March 1, 1946, the *Chief* began carrying cars for New York (conveyed east of Chicago by Pennsylvania's *Broadway Limited* and New York Central's *20th Century Limited)* and Washington,

90
SANTA FE

415
SANTA FE
90
SANTA FE
Santa F

Above, on March 26, 1950, hardly a peak travel season, *El Capitan* is a substantial, glamorous, glittery consist — twelve cars long, including two lunch-counter diners — running above Morley, Colorado, with A-B-A Alco PA's: beauty from nose to boat-tail obs. OTTO C. PERRY, DENVER PUBLIC LIBRARY, WESTERN COLLECTION

Facing page: Contrasts in postwar Santa Fe passenger railroading. Top left, Second 23, the *Grand Canyon Limited,* has an eclectic consist on October 5, 1947, wheeling west across the desert at Tejon, New Mexico, behind roller-bearing Northern No. 3784. A double-door express box car and a pair of curiously antique heavyweights are strange bedfellows for five lightweight coaches. Top right, nearly a decade later, on July 31, 1957, the *Grand Canyon* (in the hole here at Glorietta Pass, New Mexico) still shows its heavyweight/lightweight ambivalence. Bottom left, an *Indian*-series 24-duplex-roomette car, on the *Grand Canyon Limited* — a regular assignment for this fleet of twelve cars. Bottom right, "class number" PA No. 51, guest of honor at the Waldorf-Astoria inaugural party, glistens in the finery of youth. Behind these lanky Alcos is a *Scout* diner, decked out in two-tone gray with a "Scout" sign below the windows. R. S. PLUMMER, GORDON C. BASSETT COLLECTION, TOP RIGHT; SANTA FE RAILWAY, BOTTOM

SANTA FE
3784

SANTA FE

51
SANTA FE

Alco PA No. 55 is dramatically outnumbered by steam in this shop view, as workmen prepare to lift the carbody off the trucks. In spite of the numerical odds evident here, the diesel will prevail. SANTA FE RAILWAY

D.C. (conveyed by Baltimore & Ohio's *Capitol Limited)*. This innovation brought convenience for transcontinental travelers and interest for consist-watchers, since off-line Pullmans began appearing in these premier trains.

The transfer of cars among trains at Chicago was an excellent example of the now-vanished expedition with which railroads operated in those days. Westbound, at the time of the inaugural of the transcontinental Pullmans, the B&O's *Capitol Limited* was due to arrive at Chicago's Grand Central Station at 8:25 a.m. At 9:18 the *20th Century* pulled into LaSalle Street Station; last was Pennsy's *Broadway*, with its 10:00 a.m. arrival at Union Station. The *Chief*'s Chicago departure was scheduled for 12:01 p.m., which meant that the consist had to be positioned at the platform in Dearborn Station before 11:30 a.m. Thus cars had to be collected from three stations, gathered at Santa Fe's 18th Street Coach Yard, serviced and thoroughly scrubbed, and cut into the head end of the *Chief* consist, which was then backed into a fourth station, all in this brief time.

Passengers were given the option of staying aboard the cars during switching and servicing. On the inaugural westbound trip, about half of the thirty-nine passengers aboard the three through Pullmans chose to do so, while the others went off for a very brief look at the sights of Chicago. Reassembled aboard the three sleepers, at noon plus one minute they headed off for Los Angeles behind trend-setting diesel No. 167—the one FT A-B-B-A set purchased new from EMD with passenger gearing and boilers; on its success was based the conversion of the ten freight FT sets by Santa Fe.

The *Chief* was just one of a number of trains west of Chicago to handle coast-to-coast Pullmans. Also offering New York-to-Los Angeles service were Rock Island and Southern Pacific's *Golden State Limited* and Chicago & North Western and Union Pacific's *Los Angeles Limited*. To San Francisco transcontinental cars were carried on the C&NW-UP-SP *San Francisco Overland Limited* and the Chicago, Burlington & Quincy-Denver & Rio Grande Western-Western Pacific *Exposition Flyer*. Thus the shuttling of cars around Chicago between arrivals and departures was hectic and impressive.

Top left, on April 12, 1952, the eastbound *Grand Canyon* with three-unit Alco power emerges from one of the tunnels between Caliente and Bealville, California, on the joint Southern Pacific-Santa Fe line over the Tehachapi Mountains. The *Grand Canyon* was a regular assignment for the PA's. Top right, rounding the curve under Signal Bridge No. 1 on the throat tracks at Los Angeles Union Passenger Terminal is Santa Fe 4-8-2 No. 3743 with train 72, the *San Diegan.* The E1's usually assigned to this train are in for repairs today — January 27, 1948. Bottom, just a few miles from its namesake city, *San Diegan* No. 74 approaches Pacific Beach, California, on August 2, 1947, with E1's Nos. 8 and 15 and thirteen cars — the third from the head-end being a Chicago-San Diego through Pullman off the *Chief.* After being bumped from the transcontinentals by F-units, the E1's called *San Diegan*-country home, faring best on flat terrain in their old age. STAN KISTLER

Facing page: PA's followed the superannuated E1's as regular power on the *San Diegans*. Here, on Easter Sunday in 1962, PA's 69 and 76 whisk an eight-car consist along the Pacific shore at San Clemente. STAN KISTLER. Left, PA's lead a southbound *San Diegan* through Rose Canyon; below, F-units later worked the *San Diegan,* as here, again at San Clemente. SANTA FE RAILWAY

Some unusual sleepers participated in through service, many of them wearing the two-tone-gray Pullman pool colors. Santa Fe's 6-section 6-roomette 4-double-bedroom smooth-sided *Valley*-series cars (P-S, 1942) held down the *Chief*'s Washington-Los Angeles line. Pennsy dressed five 4-compartment 2-drawing-room 2-double-bedroom sleepers—*Imperial Park, Pass, Point, Range,* and *Terrace* (P-S, 1938)—in Pullman grays for transcontinental service. And New York Central sent west a variety of its own gray smooth-sided, Pullman-Standard cars, most commonly *Cascade*-series 10-roomette 5-double-bedroom cars. To fill out the L.A.-New York pool, Santa Fe contributed the only stainless-steel cars in the service, Indian-named 4-compartment 2-drawing-room 4-double-bedroom sleepers built for the *Chief* or the *Super Chief*.

Transcontinental sleepers and courier-nurses were attractive features that Santa Fe could offer with existing prewar equipment. To promote these and other good services already in place, an ad campaign was launched to reach 65 million people via *Life, Collier's, Saturday Evening Post,* and other magazines, as well as newspapers throughout the country. Chico, the little Indian boy created by the advertising department, was featured throughout the ads.

But the major expansions and improvements had to wait for the flood of new sleepers, coaches, lounges, and diners that would finally gush forth from the carbuilders once the war-created log jam had broken. This new array of stainless steel allowed culmination of an evolutionary direction more than a decade in development: daily operation of the *Super Chief* and *El Capitan*.

On February 29, 1948, those premier, extra-fare streamliners finally attained that status—doubling the every-other-day frequency which had been in place since September 1946. (Competitor UP had moved its *City of Los Angeles* to daily back on April 27, 1947; slow delivery of new equipment held up AT&SF.) At the same time the trains were largely re-equipped, giving the Santa Fe ample excuse to mark the event with equipment displays and banquets. Furthermore, AT&SF had decreed its passage of the hundred-million-mile mark of diesel operation, stirring this into the celebratory broth. Luncheons were held in both Los Angeles and Chicago to note the dual occasion.

Fred G. Gurley, then president of the Santa Fe, spoke at both. At the Chicago luncheon, held in the Grand Ballroom of the Palmer House, Gurley put the present events in the context of the inauguration of the experimental, heavyweight *Super Chief* back in 1936, the depths of the Depression. "Our passenger revenues that year were only 40 percent of what they had been in 1929, the year of the stock-market collapse," he said. "We had experienced traffic diversions to the splendid highways financed substantially by government, and the fostering attitude toward air transportation which later became so pronounced was then apparent."

Then came the good news: "The complete reversal of our passenger traffic picture has been the most amazing experience of my life. Santa Fe passenger revenues in 1947 were 220 percent more than in the year when the first *Super Chief* started as a once-a-week experiment." For the future: "We are now engaged in purchasing 152 additional passenger cars. The average cost is more than a hundred thousand dollars per car. . . ."

Entertainment at both luncheons featured dances and songs by five Indian tribes: Apache, Hopi, Jemez, Navajo, and Zuni. In Chicago, tenor James Melton served as emcee and sang. In Los Angeles, Bob Hope was master of ceremonies. But the trains themselves, of course, were the real focus of interest. They were exhibited in Dearborn Station Annex on February 26, the day of the Chicago luncheon, and at Los Angeles Union Passenger Terminal two days later.

Facing page: On March 26, 1950, No. 20, the eastbound *Chief,* glides through farming country near Trinidad, Colorado, powered by F3 set No. 23. Behind the two lightweight baggage cars is a heavyweight baggage-lounge — "shadow-lined" in the paint shop to match the fluted stainless-steel cars. When the *Super Chief* went daily in 1948, it required all available 1380-class baggage-dormitory-lounges, some of which previously had run on the *Chief*; thus heavyweights 1300-1305 returned to *Chief* consists for a time. Immediately behind the baggage-lounge is an off-line Pullman — one of four transcontinental sleepers carried by the *Chief* at this time. Two went to New York Central's *20th Century Limited* for New York, one to the Pennsy's *Broadway,* also to New York, and one to Baltimore & Ohio's *Capitol Limited* for Washington. OTTO C. PERRY, DENVER PUBLIC LIBRARY, WESTERN HISTORY COLLECTION.
Santa Fe's *Valley*-series 6-section 6-roomette 4-double-bedroom sleepers (built by Pullman-Standard in 1942) were regularly assigned to this Washington line. Right, these smooth-sided cars are seen in three garbs: *Estancia Valley* in the original, two-tone gray (top); *Paradise Valley* in shadow-lining in a *Capitol Limited* consist on the B&O at Silver Spring, Maryland (middle); and *Tesuque Valley* in solid gray with silver roof, the last scheme, at Chicago in July 1961. JOSEPH W. SHINE, ROBERT J. WAYNER COLLECTION, TOP; PETER TILP COLLECTION, MIDDLE AND BOTTOM

For the most part the consists on display were new. The *Super Chief*'s Pullmans, for instance, were fresh from the builder. The era on the Santa Fe of individual, unpronouncable Indian Pullman names had closed, giving way to the series naming usual on other railroads. (Pullman had strongly encouraged this direction.) To re-equip the *Super,* Pullman-Standard delivered seventeen 4-compartment 2-drawing-room 4-double-bedroom *Regal*-series cars (*Regal Center* to *Regal Vale*); nineteen 10-roomette 2-compartment 3-double-bedroom *Blue*-series cars (*Blue Jay* to *Blue Water*), a configuration unique to Santa Fe; and 4-drawing-room 1-double-bedroom lounge-observations *Vista Canyon, Vista Cavern, Vista Heights,* and *Vista Valley*. The additional obs to cover the five consists needed to hold down daily *Super Chief* service was the similarly configured prewar *Chief* observation *Coconino*, renamed *Vista Plains*. Along with a *Vista* car, each consist contained three *Regal* sleepers and three *Blue* sleepers.

In addition to the Pullmans, each *Super Chief* included a new 1390-series dormitory-club lounge. The 36-seat diners and the baggage-barber shop-buffet lounges that headed the train were prewar cars.

The new equipment incorporated such improve-

Below, this enticing *Super Chief* ad traded on the train's glamor and prestige — an approach the Santa Fe had used ever since the snooty ads for the *de-Luxe* back in the teens. The car featured is a *Vista*-series sleeper-observation. Right, such a car carried the *Super Chief* drumhead in Albuquerque on March 7, 1952. STAN KISTLER, RIGHT

Below, thousands of envelopes bearing this cachet were carried aboard the first daily *Super Chief* in 1948; they were postmarked in both Chicago and Los Angeles. Similar envelopes were carried aboard *El Cap.* Facing page: Excerpts from a booklet touting the daily *Super Chief.* SANTA FE RAILWAY

ments as non-fogging windows; toilets and washbasins enclosed in annexes rather than exposed as previously in bedrooms and compartments; increased insulation for a quieter ride; and wiring throughout the train for sound. In each bedroom, compartment, roomette, and drawing room was a panel with push buttons, allowing the passenger to select wire-recorded music (one channel for popular, one for semi-classical), a radio program (just one was tuned into the system at any given point of the journey), or public-address announcements. Above this button a panel lit up to alert the passenger when an announcement was about to be made. To prevent disturbance of neighbors, the sound system could be turned on only with the door to the room closed. There were also separate wire-recorded music systems in the diner (with different programs for lunch and for dinner) and in the club lounge.

There was new equipment for *El Capitan,* too, some of which had actually entered service the previous summer. Making up the fourteen-car consists standard when this deluxe coach train went to daily service were, in addition to a storage mail car and a baggage-dormitory, eight 44-seat chair cars; two lunch-counter diners; a club-lounge car; and a chair-observation. All the 44-seat coaches (built by Pullman-Standard) were new and roomier than the 52-seat cars they replaced; new also were the Budd-built lunch-counter diners and Pullman-Standard club lounges. Among the coach-observations that covered the service, three were new 40-seaters from P-S and three were 38-seat rebuilds of prewar Budd cars.

The new chair cars featured Ride Master seats, with foam-rubber cushions molded to body measurements, full leg rests that tucked under the seats when not in use, and upholstered armrests with finger-tip controls releasing the seat backs to three different reclining positions. Window spacing was rearranged for better vision. Floors were carpeted. Walls and ceilings were pastel-toned and accented by soft indirect lighting. There was also a direct light over each seat. Wire-recorded music, which played discreetly throughout the train, was introduced later in the year.

At the center of the consist was a full-length lounge car, providing a convivial meeting place for passengers. This colorful car had a variety of divans, tables, and chairs, a bar, and a writing desk stocked with stationery bearing the train's logo. These lounges and the new coaches were decorated by Ralph Harmon in

The Club Lounge Car

Floor plan

CLUB LOUNGE CAR

The Club Lounge, near the center of the train and adjoining the diner, provides a gay, cheery meeting place for passengers, with that high degree of luxurious comfort and opportunity for leg stretching and relaxation peculiar to this fine train.

In the Club Lounge are a cocktail bar, writing desk with stationery, and a profusion of current periodicals and papers. Lounge chairs and sofas are specially designed for roomy restful comfort.

Music from special wire recordings, radio programs and messages from the train announcement system, have been carefully planned, in this car, so that they will not interfere with conversation or reading, but yet will be loud enough to be enjoyed by those wishing to listen.

The romance of the early Spanish explorers and western pioneers still lingers along the Santa Fe Route through the Southwest. Gallup, Canyon Diablo, Flagstaff, Cajon Pass, Needles and all along the way the Super Chief rolls through a region rich in romance of the past.

The Dining Car

Floor plan

DINING CAR SERVICE FRED HARVEY

For more than half a century discriminating travelers have recognized Fred Harvey dining car service on the Santa Fe as outstanding in the transportation world. Fred Harvey food has always meant food well chosen, attractively prepared and carefully served. This famous service reaches its finest expression in the beautiful "dining-room-on-wheels" of the new Super Chief, with its carefully chosen personnel, its gleaming silver and glassware, snowy napery and especially designed china.

Breakfast and luncheon are served a la carte; dinner, both a la carte and table d'hote.

The golden west is best typified by its vast citrus groves that stretch for miles along the Santa Fe Route. Aboard the Super Chief passengers delight at the sight of these great orchards as they travel through California.

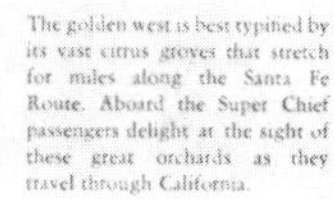

The Drawing Room

Floor plan arrangement for nighttime

DRAWING ROOMS

Spacious comfort keynotes the tastefully decorated Drawing Rooms on the new Super Chief.

By day the Drawing Room provides two lounge chairs and a lounge sofa. At night the sofa becomes a bed, another bed materializes from the wall, and an upper berth is available if desired. There is a complete toilet annex and a large enclosed wardrobe, ample luggage storage and shoe box, as well as many other features, to make the drawing room the most desirable of all train accommodations.

Non-fogging windows, improved lighting, and individually controlled air-conditioning and ventilation are modern improvements,

Radio, special music from wire recordings, and train announcements, operate by push-button control at the pleasure of the passenger.

Along your way via Super Chief you will see many fine products of Indian handicraft. *Rug weaving*—a native art of the Navajos started when explorers brought in sheep from Spain to provide the Indians with their first wool.

The Observation Lounge

Floor plan

OBSERVATION LOUNGE

From the broad windows of the Observation Lounge passengers can enjoy sweeping views of the passing scenery and relax in comfortable lounge chairs, or browse through a wide selection of current periodicals. A writing desk with distinctive stationery is an invitation to write about your trip, and your trip via Santa Fe is really "something to write home about." Here, too, soft music lends atmosphere to the colorful decoration of this beautiful car.

The beautiful Observation Lounge is the rear car of the Super Chief and supplements the Forward Lounge and Club Lounge in providing the generous extra space for relaxation and "moving around" that is so much enjoyed by rail travelers.

Indian ceremonials at Gallup, and at various places throughout the Navajo, Hopi and Pueblo Indian reservations, are unusual and interesting events. • Prayers rise to the gods, when dancers nod beaked headdresses and wave plumed arms in the ceremony of the Eagle Dance.

Top left, Cajon Pass, March 1948; top right, Alco RS's helping F's on *El Capitan* climbing Raton Pass near Wootton, Colorado, July 1954. Left, F3 No. 17 leads first 24, the *Grand Canyon,* at Cajon in September 1947. STAN KISTLER, TOP LEFT; RICHARD H. KINDIG, TOP RIGHT; ROBERT F. COLLINS, LEFT

what he called "canyon colors"; upholstery, draperies, paints, metals, and woods all reflected the feeling of the Southwest.

The lunch-counter diners were the only new non-Pullman-Standard cars in the consist. Built by Budd, they were styled by Henry Dreyfuss, the industrial designer perhaps best known for his classic 1938 edition of the *20th Century Limited*. For *El Cap*'s lunch-counter diners, he created a color combination reminiscent of Navajo sand painting: "copper, wine, and green of the Canyon, the blue of a Navajo's robe, the gold of a cottonwood along the Rio Grande, the true azure of the sky," according to *The Santa Fe Magazine*.

Aboard the first daily runs of the *Super Chief* and *El Capitan,* the Santa Fe offered to carry envelopes on which it impressed cachets for stamp collectors. Since the trains had no Railway Post Office cars, these imprinted envelopes—which bore the train's logo, the image of a diesel streamliner, and the notation "Commemorating inaugural of daily service Chicago to Los

A Conquistador (left) adorned the cover of a postwar brochure touting *El Capitan.* Below are excerpts from that booklet. SANTA FE RAILWAY

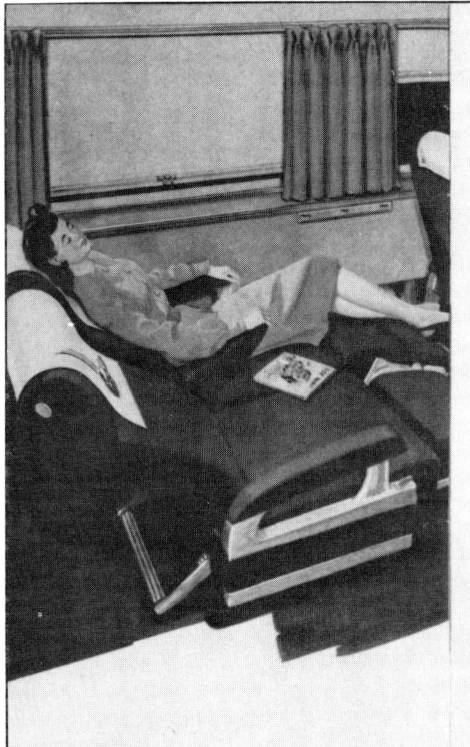

● The Ride Master seats aboard El Capitan provide every feature for restful travel, day and night.

Built with foam-rubber cushions, the seats are molded to body measurements for greater riding comfort.

The leg rests are conveniently built under the seats and can readily be pulled out when needed for use in reclining or sitting position.

Upholstered armrests contain finger-tip controls that release back of seat to three different reclining positions, and at your finger tips you will also find an ash tray built into the seat.

Of course, all seats aboard El Capitan are reserved in advance to assure you a carefree trip.

Ah-h-h, what comfort!

The new Ride Master seat reclined to full position, with leg rest extended, providing a luxury of comfort.

● This friendly young woman aboard El Capitan is a capable, registered nurse.

Her duties are to lend a helping hand to mothers traveling with babies and children, to aid the sick and aged, and to assist all travelers requiring her services.

Besides her professional ability the Courier-Nurse can bring to interested travelers a personal knowledge of scenes along the route of El Capitan, for she has visited the many scenic attractions in the colorful Santa Fe Southwest.

You'll like the Courier-Nurse

The Courier-Nurse on El Capitan is a registered nurse attending all passengers requiring her capable and friendly service.

Passengers catch a glimpse of the colorful Indians of the Southwest when El Capitan makes its brief stop at Albuquerque.

Angeles"—were cancelled by postal authorities in Chicago or Los Angeles, then loaded aboard the inaugural runs. Approximately 22,000 cachets were carried.

With the *Super* and *El Cap* both rolling daily, Santa Fe had reached a major milestone. The next came just a little more than a month later with the inauguration of a new train, the Chicago-Galveston *Texas Chief*. This PA-powered consist was in the glamorous mode of the other *Chiefs* and embodied many of the features of its transcontinental tribesmen: courier-nurse service, Fred Harvey Meals, 44-seat coaches with Ride Master seats, and wire-recorded music throughout the train.

Though lunch-counter diners apparently provided the meal service in the very beginning, these were quickly replaced by standard 36-seat diners. These cars, as well as the mid-train club lounge-dormitories (with former barber shop converted to steward's room), had been built in 1938 for the streamlining of the *Chief*. Sleeping accommodations offered were sections, standard roomettes, duplex roomettes, bedrooms, compartments, and drawing rooms. Sleeper lines, in addition to Chicago-Galveston, were Chicago-Oklahoma City, Chicago-Wichita, and Chicago-Tulsa (on the *Oil Flyer* beyond Kansas City). Because so many sleepers had to be cut in and out of the consist, the *Texas Chief* lacked an observation car—becoming the first Santa Fe streamliner to operate without this sign of cachet. It didn't even carry a drumhead.

One train remained to complete the burst of postwar streamliner additions: the *Kansas City Chief*, an overnight service between Chicago and Kansas City. Inaugurated on April 12, 1950, the train had a basically lightweight consist, with 44-seat Ride Master coaches and sleepers offering sections, duplex and standard roomettes, bedrooms, and compartments. However, the most interesting cars were heavyweights; named "Centennial Club" in honor of Kansas City's one-hundredth anniversary, these snack diner-lounges, rebuilt from coaches, were decorated in plush Victorian splendor. Within three years, though, the Centennial Clubs (one for each of the two consists required to protect the service) were withdrawn, replaced by separate lunch-counter diners and bar-lounge-dormitories.

Facing page: *Texas Chief* interiors. The lounge shown was used in the Dallas section. Top left, eastbound for Kansas City and Chicago, the *Texas Chief* passes Dalton Junction, meeting point for the main from Fort Worth and Galveston and a new Dallas line. Top right, the westbound *Texas Chief* winds through the broken countryside near Washita Canyon. Bottom, the westbound *Texas Chief* crosses the Washita River near Gene Autry, Oklahoma. SANTA FE RAILWAY, BOTH PAGES

(Scheduled for business travel, the train in both directions left at 10 p.m. and arrived before 8 a.m., so the only meals served were early breakfasts.)

When inaugurated, the *Kansas City Chief* complemented the daytime *Kansas Cityan/Chicagoan* streamliners. But the traveler between those cities could also ride the *Super Chief, El Capitan,* the *Chief,* the *Texas Chief,* the *Grand Canyon,* or the *California Limited*—truly an impressive array of options. As the fifties began, the Santa Fe passenger fleet—dominated by the glamorous streamliners, but with some important heavyweight consists still in place as well—was remarkable in both quality and quantity. But the railroad still had some notable improvements and even additions to unveil in the next decade.

Top left, the menu from the *Kansas City Chief*'s "Centennial Club" — from July 1950, very early in the train's career — offered a choice of "Ginger Ale, Canada Dry" or "Ginger Ale, Fred Harvey Dry," as well as Fred Harvey club soda. There were ham, cheese, ox tongue, and bacon and egg sandwiches, in addition to the basic beverages, hard and soft. Top right, the handsome period interior of the "Centennial Club" lounge. Left, a timetable cover from the train's second year of service. PETER TILP COLLECTION, TOP LEFT; SANTA FE RAILWAY, ROBERT J. WAYNER COLLECTION, TOP RIGHT; SANTA FE RAILWAY, LEFT

Right, *Navajo,* the original lightweight *Super Chief* observation, served the *Chief* later in its career, as here at San Bernardino, California. Below, the *Golden Gate* begins its flight up the San Joaquin Valley as it clears the westbound yard lead at Bakersfield, California, with rebuilt E8M Nos. 80 and 80A, plus an F7B and fourteen cars on October 18, 1953. Earlier that year the Santa Fe's fleet of by-then-obsolete E1's had been remanufactured into these 2000-horsepower E8M's, similar in appearance to ordinary production-run E8's. SANTA FE RAILWAY, RIGHT; STAN KISTLER, BELOW

6

Domes and Hi-Levels

In the early morning hours, the Hi-Level *El Capitan* pauses at Barstow, California. The wide brick platform of the handsome station is dense with Railway Express Agency wagons, some heavily laden with mail and express. SANTA FE RAILWAY

The last great gala feast in American passenger railroading was served under glass—the glass of the Vista-Domes, Astra-Domes, Scenic-Domes, Planetarium Domes, Pleasure Domes, Big Domes, Super Domes, and Great Domes that arrived in the late forties through the mid-fifties. With these spectacular cars, the railroads of the West—for restrictive clearances precluded their use in the East—made one final dramatic bid to keep passengers from deserting to automobiles and airplanes.

The modern dome car was conceived in July 1944 by Cyrus R. Osborn, a General Motors vice-president. The idea came to him while he rode the Denver & Rio Grande Western's scenic line through Glenwood Canyon in Colorado aboard one of his company's FT's. In the spring of 1945 GM was displaying drawings and models of its projected "Astra Liner" at an exhibit for railroad executives. But by July of that year Burlington had taken one of its Budd-built stainless-steel coaches and turned it into the prototype *Silver Dome,* doing the conversion in its own Aurora, Illinois, shops.

By the end of the year forty dome cars were on order with various builders. The first to enter revenue service were coaches and parlor-lounge-observations delivered by Budd in the fall of 1947 for Burlington's *Twin Cities Zephyrs*. Earlier that year, in May, Pullman-Standard had completed some domes for General Motors, which became the four-car demonstrator *Train of Tomorrow*. In the consist were a dome dining car, dome sleeper, dome chair car, and dome tavern-observation. (Santa Fe competitor Union Pacific eventually bought these cars.)

Unlike the Budd cars and domes subsequently delivered by American Car & Foundry, which had curved glass in their domes, Pullman-Standard's *Train of Tomorrow* cars—and most domes to come from that builder subsequently—had flat glass, giving them a distinctive if somewhat angular appearance. Into this genre fell the Santa Fe's first domes: the Pleasure Domes built by P-S for the *Super Chief* and introduced in January 1951 as the highlight of another virtually complete re-equipping of the flagship. Remarkably, this was the third re-equipping of the train in the six short years since World War II.

The Pleasure Dome—its floor plan a virtual copy of the *Train of Tomorrow*'s dome-lounges—had a number of unique features, most notably the first private dining room aboard a train. Called the Turquoise Room, this space seated twelve and was available for private luncheon, cocktail, or dinner parties. The Turquoise Room could be booked through the dining-car steward or through traffic representatives in advance of travel. (When not reserved for private parties, the room was available for all passengers.)

The decorative keynote of the room was a reproduction of a silver-accented turquoise medallion, dis-

Below, publicity for the new Pullman-Standard Pleasure Dome; Right, a photographic portrait of the car. PETER TILP COLLECTION, BELOW; SANTA FE RAILWAY, RIGHT

2 The Dome Lounge—"top of the Super, next to the stars"

1 The Turquoise Room is a distinctive private dining room for Super Chief travelers. Nine persons can be served and when not reserved for private parties, all passengers may enjoy this room for relaxation and refreshments.

TURQUOISE ROOM

AND PLEASURE DOME LOUNGE CAR

TURQUOISE ROOM

1 2 3 4

4 The Main Lounge—spacious and comfortable

3 The Lower Lounge—colorful, intimate and inviting.

played in a shadow box on the forward wall. Carpeting was turquoise blue; gold-tinted mirrors lined the side walls, and gold-colored draperies framed the windows opposite. China, silver, and linens were of special, exclusive design.

The Turquoise Room could be entered from the main corridor or from the lower cocktail lounge, under the dome. This was a smart room with *tete-de-negre*-colored carpeting and cherry-red curtains and bar-front quilting. Flesh-tinted mirrors gave a feeling of spaciousness, without destroying the atmosphere of cozy intimacy.

The largest area aboard the car was the main lounge, an inviting place for socializing or watching the scenery roll by. Two sofas, several lounge chairs, and a built-in seating unit were carefully designed for unobstructed viewing. The warm colors of the southwestern desert predominated: beige walls, creamy yellow ceiling, upholstery in arch green and terra cotta. Draperies showed a California seashell pattern.

The same color scheme extended upstairs to the dome, which had a unique seating plan. In the middle section were eight revolving parlor-car-type seats.

Left, for a time in the mid-fifties, Indian guides in tribal costumes rode the eastbound *Super Chief* and westbound *El Capitan* to explain landmarks and history of the Southwest to passengers. Here Harry Nieto, known as War Bow among his fellow tribesmen at Zuni pueblo in New Mexico, is in the *Super Chief*'s Pleasure Dome pointing out the famous Red Cliffs, near Gallup, New Mexico. This picture is taken looking forward, showing an unusual feature of the car: entry stairs at the front of the dome. Below is a view — this one looking backward, toward the music speaker — of the dome area after refurbishing in 1957. SANTA FE RAILWAY, LEFT; SANTA FE RAILWAY, ROBERT J. WAYNER COLLECTION, BELOW

Flanking them fore and aft were coach-type double seats—the forward ones facing forward, the rearward ones rearward. The oversized parlor seats were particularly comfortable and could be pivoted for ideal viewing angles—but, on the negative side, they reduced the dome's seating capacity to sixteen, compared to twenty-four in the typical four-across fixed-seat short dome. The Pleasure Domes, Nos. 500-505, were originally to have carried names—*Plaza Acoma, Plaza Laguna, Plaza Lamy, Plaza Santa Fe, Plaza Taos,* and *Plaza Zuni*—but these were dropped prior to the cars' entry into service.

Companion cars to the Pleasure Domes were 36-seat diners Nos. 600-606, also Pullman-Standard products, delivered in November and December of 1950. (Because of the greater maintenance requirements of dining cars, a seventh, extra car was ordered.) From the time they were delivered until well into the Amtrak era, the dining cars and dome-lounges remained inseparable—always coupled together so the Turquoise Room had access to food from the diner's kitchen. They were the emblematic cars of the *Super Chief*'s last two decades.

The re-equipped *Super Chief* of 1951 had new sleep-

The Turquoise Room as built (top right) and as remodeled in 1957 (middle right). Left, the main lounge of the Pleasure Dome after its 1957 refurbishing. SANTA FE RAILWAY, ROBERT J. WAYNER COLLECTION

Super Chief on the double horseshoe curve near Ribera, New Mexico. SANTA FE RAILWAY

ers as well. From December 1949 through March 1950, Budd had delivered twenty-seven 10-roomette 6-double-bedroom Pullmans, *Pine Arroyo* through *Pine Shore*. Later, in June and July of 1951, American Car & Foundry added thirteen 10/6's, *Palm Arch* to *Palm View*. In September through November 1950, also from ACF, had come fifteen 4-compartment 4-double-bedroom 2-drawing-room sleepers, *Regal*-series cars. The 10-roomette 2-compartment 3-double-bedroom *Blue*-series cars were withdrawn from the *Super*, replaced by *Palm*- and *Pine*-series 10/6's.

The P-S *Regal* cars from 1947 and 1948 remained, supplemented by ACF's 1950 contribution to that series. One additional 4-drawing-room 1-double-bedroom lounge-observation—*Vista Club*— was provided by ACF in November 1950, joining its sisters already on hand. Rounding out each consist was a dormitory buffet-lounge, one of six delivered in October and November 1950 by Pullman-Standard.

Throughout January 1951, this new equipment was exhibited in seven cities—Chicago, Kansas City, Los Angeles, Beverly Hills, Pasadena, San Diego, and San Bernardino. Approximately 35,000 visitors boarded the cars on this tour. "You are cordially invited to a preview of the Turquoise Room on the New Super Chief," read a special invitation to the Chicago display. "Four to seven o'clock, January 9, 1951." The cars were parked for the occasion on Michigan Boulevard, adjacent to the Tribune Tower.

Educational tours for Santa Fe's passenger people—to acquaint them with the new equipment's appointments, accommodations, and services—were operated from Los Angeles and Chicago. Then, on January 28, the re-equipped *Super Chief* entered revenue service, ushering in the era of the dome car on the Santa Fe.

Almost immediately the renewed train came by some remarkable publicity through the release of the movie "Three for Bedroom C," starring Gloria Swanson. The film, which premiered on June 12, 1952, at the Paramount Theater in Kansas City, takes place entirely on board the *Super Chief*, except for scenes at Chicago's Dearborn and the stations at Albuquerque and Pasadena.

To shoot the film, Brenco Pictures Corporation rented from Santa Fe four Pullmans, a diner, a Pleasure Dome car (all from the sixth, standby consist of the *Super*, so regular service was not affected) and a diesel. The studio dismantled the interiors of the cars at Santa Fe's Eighth Street Coach Yards in Los Angeles and hauled them to the studio, where they were put back together. Thousands of items—parts and furnishings—were removed, catalogued, and reassembled, a substantial undertaking but one that assured authenticity. The leased F-unit was used in the exterior scenes at the stations.

The unexceptional plot of this comedy involves an atomic scientist who boards the *Super Chief* at Dearborn to find his accommodation, Bedroom C, already occupied by a movie actress and her young daughter, who had been unable to get reservations and so had stowed away. He, therefore, moves into the men's lounge. The scientist and actress begin a romance which, though troubled by the appearance of her agent and a new leading man, ends happily. Meanwhile, the moviegoer is treated to a panorama of *Super Chief* delights, with scenes taking place in various Pullman rooms, the diner, the barber shop, and the Turquoise Room.

Relishing the unprecedented publicity gold mine that "Three for Bedroom C" represented, Santa Fe shared prominently in the hoopla attending the movie's opening. A parade from Kansas City Union Station to the theater for the premier was led by a miniature Santa Fe train; following in a fleet of convertibles were the star and her "court"—a dozen attractive women chosen from among Santa Fe employees. The railroad gave Miss Swanson a silver-plated diesel locomotive throttle on a plaque inscribed: "We open the Super Chief throttle to full speed to symbolize our wish for success and future happiness for our friend and shining star. . . ." After the premier, activity shifted to Chicago where the real *Super* served as a background for photographs and the scene of a gathering for the press. Then Miss Swanson boarded the train for L. A.—a rolling promotion, as press representatives from Los Angeles, Phoenix, and Winslow, Arizona, joined the train at Albuquerque to ride west with the star.

All this redounded greatly to Santa Fe's benefit. The upbeat movie showed the railroad's glamorous flagship at its most luxurious and romantic. In fact, some of the columnists and critics found the *Super Chief* at least as captivating as the movie or its star. And perhaps most notable of all in retrospect, "Three for Bedroom C" is remarkable testimony to Warner Brothers' confidence as late as 1952 that the passenger train—or at least the movie industry's own particular darling, the *Super Chief*—had the drawing power to bring the public to the theater.

Just the month before "Three for Bedroom C" premiered, Santa Fe had made a service improvement in movieland. On May 21, 1952, a pair of Budd Rail Diesel Cars were put into service on the Surf Line between Los Angeles and San Diego, making two daily round trips—one non-stop, one with three firm and six flag stops. Added to a pair of round trips made by the *San Diegan* streamliners (with eight-car consists, expandable by three coaches on weekends) and one made by a heavyweight local, this RDC service increased the Los Angeles-San Diego frequency to seven.

The Budd Cars, the only ones Santa Fe ever owned, were RDC-1's—the all-passenger version, with no mail or baggage facilities—seating eighty passengers. On the non-stop run, for which there was a fifty-cent surcharge, all seats were reserved.

A test run for representatives of the California Public Utilities Commission was made on May 19, and on May 20 San Diego business, civic, and military leaders were invited aboard a special demonstration trip. The inaugural on May 21 launched the Budd Cars auspiciously into San Diego-Los Angeles service—a stint that would end less than four years later in catastrophe when, on January 22, 1956, running as No. 82, the cars overturned at high speed at Redondo Junction, near Los Angeles, killing thirty.

After that the cars were sent anonymously and ignominously to Kansas City where—with one of them rebuilt to baggage-coach configuration—they plied in unnamed local service until 1965. Then they were shifted to take over the El Paso-to-Albuquerque *El Pasoan*—a diminutive consist when conventionally equipped, notable in its inclusion for a time of the one-of-a-kind "Lunch-o-Mat" car and, later, drumhead-carrying parlor-observation No. 3240 (built in 1938 for the *San Diegan*). The RDC's closed out *El Pasoan* service—the train was discontinued on April 9, 1968—before being sold to the Baltimore & Ohio in 1970.

But Budd had much bigger things brewing for Santa Fe in the mid fifties than a pair of RDC's, things which would be revealed early in 1954. The first news of that year, however, was service changes involving the *Chief*. January 10 was a momentous occasion, for on that date the historic train lost its all-Pullman status, owned since birth in 1926, with the addition to its consist of four 48-seat coaches and a lunch-counter diner to serve them. At the same time, its transcontinental sleepers were shifted to the *Super Chief*, and its schedule shortened by over four hours eastbound and five and one-half westbound. Further, extra-fare charges on the *Chief* and *El Capitan* were eliminated, and on the *Super Chief* reduced from $15.00 to $7.50.

This added up to mixed news at best, but the revelations from The Budd Company would be all good. On February 10, in the carbuilder's home city of Philadelphia, Budd unveiled the first of Santa Fe's fleet of fourteen "Big Domes"—eight for *El Capitan* and the *Chicagoan/Kansas Cityan* and six for the soon-to-be-inaugurated *San Francisco Chief*. The two types of Big Domes varied little; they shared an upper-level configuration of fifty-seven coach seats and an 18-seat lounge. The first series delivered—Nos. 506-513, for *El Cap* and *Chicagoan/Kansas Cityan*—had a 28-seat bar lounge and a room for the courier-nurse downstairs. Nos. 550-555, for the *San Francisco Chief*, had on the lower level a much smaller lounge, which left room for a crew dormitory sleeping twelve.

Though not the first to operate full-length domes—Pullman-Standard had delivered ten to The Milwaukee Road in late 1952 for the *Morning, Afternoon,* and *Olympian Hiawatha*s—Santa Fe would always be in an elite group with its Big Domes. For Great North-

Bottom, the Santa Fe's lone RDC pair as built — configured as RDC1's. Top, in this June 6, 1965, view at the Sand Creek engine terminal at Newton, Kansas — a week before the RDC's ceased running over the Middle Division between Newton and Great Bend — No. 192 shows its configuration as rebuilt in July 1956: 36-seat-baggage. STEVE PATTERSON, TOP; SANTA FE RAILWAY, BOTTOM

Above, Big Dome 507, one of eight built for *El Capitan* and *Chicagoan/Kansas Cityan* service. Left, the lounge area on the upper level of one of these cars. (Note the bottles of Santa Fe/Fred Harvey's own ginger ale.) SANTA FE RAILWAYS. Facing page: *El Capitan* on Cajon Pass on March 7, 1954, is a mighty classy train, sporting both an observation car and brand-new Big Dome. STAN KISTLER

ern's *Empire Builder*, Budd in 1955 would provide six Great Domes—virtually identical to Santa Fe's Big Domes, but with a slightly expanded lower lounge allowed by the absence of a nurse's room—and beginning in July of 1954 Southern Pacific would outshop seven low-profile domes; technically three-quarter length domes, these were rebuilds from conventional single-level cars.

That completed the roster of full-length dome cars: thirty-seven in all, with Santa Fe ranking first in numbers owned, with fourteen. They were an equipment development which came very late in the era of passenger-car purchases by private railroads. Though this is no doubt the main reason for their scarcity, they were not generally regarded as unmitigated successes. That large an area under glass was not easy to keep

The *San Francisco Chief,* inaugurated June 1954, is shown here near Franklin Tunnel, passing a hillside covered with California Poppies. A baggage car and four coaches lead off the consist; behind, not visible, are Big Dome, diner, and sleepers. SANTA FE RAILWAY

cool, and the cars lacked the unobstructed forward vision of the short domes.

But Santa Fe's Big Domes *were* dazzling, exciting cars when they rolled off the line at Budd. The main seating area, at the front of the upper level, had coach-type seats angled ten degrees from forward for better visibility. To the rear was the cocktail lounge, with a small service bar connected by electric dumbwaiter to the lower level. The lounge's Lucite tables, with feathery sprays of Australian seaweed embedded in them, were indirectly illuminated by lights under the tables' built-in ashtrays. This produced soft, unobtrusive lighting for those in the lounge, with no distracting glare to bother the sightseers forward, where the lights would be turned out for better viewing. The "Starlite" lighting system throughout the upper level was designed to provide the light necessary at night without compromising the view. In the lower-level lounge were seats for twenty-eight (ten in the 550-series cars for the *San Francisco Chief*), a writing desk, and a service bar.

Decoratively, the Big Domes continued AT&SF's reliance on the colors and designs of the southwestern Indians. Pueblo beige, Zuni turquoise, and mesa red colored walls and ceilings throughout; coach seats on the upper level were upholstered in a rust-colored needlepoint fabric, and those in both lounges in straw-colored Naugahyde. All carpeting was of a prickly-pear-cactus design in charcoal, beige, and turquoise, created exclusively for Santa Fe.

The lower-level lounge of the 506-series cars had as room dividers four edge-lighted double Lucite panels etched with Kachina dolls, authentic hand-painted illustrations of idols worshipped by the Navajo and Hopi Indians. Hand-hammered copper repousses of Indian design provided further ornamentation. The cars contained a sound system for radio, wire-recorded music, and public-address announcements.

After being displayed around the system, Big Domes Nos. 506-513 entered service on *El Capitan* March 1, and on the *Chicagoan/Kansas Cityan* later that month. Nos. 550-555 came along from Budd shortly thereafter. They would be the keynote cars of a wholly new service, perhaps the last major passenger train to be launched in America by any railroad: the *San Francisco Chief*.

Remarkably, the Santa Fe had never had a through service from the Midwest to the San Francisco Bay area. The new train's streamlined competitors had gotten there long before. The *City of San Francisco* began running in 1936 and the *California Zephyr* in 1949, and both had heavyweight predecessors. Santa Fe's willingness to enter this competition so late was an impressive statement of the railroad's abiding faith in the passenger train.

The *San Francisco Chief* was begun with little new equipment—just its flamboyant Big Dome bar-lounge dormitories and its mundane 48-seat coaches, from among a forty-five-car order delivered by Budd in late 1953. Its Pullmans were all on the existing roster: a 24-duplex-roomette car in the *Indian* series, a *Pine*- or *Palm*-series 10/6, a *Blue*-series 10-roomette 2-compartment 3-double-bedroom car, a *Regal*-series 4-compartment 2-drawing-room 4-double-bedroom car, an Indian-named 8-section 2-compartment 2-double-bedroom sleeper. The 36-seat diners dated from 1937 and had been part of the first streamlined *Chief*. The lunch-counter diner-dormitories, however, were much newer, having come from Pullman-Standard in 1950.

Right, *San Francisco Chief* entering Muir Tunnel in California. Far right, two sleeper-lounge-observations rebuilt for mid-train service and used on the *San Francisco Chief*: *Chaistla* (top) and *Vista Valley* (bottom). SANTA FE RAILWAY, RIGHT AND FAR RIGHT TOP; PETER TILP, FAR RIGHT BOTTOM

Though most of its cars were hand-me-downs, and though it was targeted to serve intermediate markets rather than aiming strictly for endpoint-to-endpoint business (as had most of Santa Fe's earlier long-haul streamliners), there was nothing second-rate about this new Oakland-Chicago train. Unique among the streamliners in running over the Southern District, through Amarillo, Texas, and Clovis, New Mexico, while the *Super, El Cap,* and *Grand Canyon* plied the Northern District, via La Junta, Colorado, and Albuquerque, the *San Francisco Chief* offered courier-nurse service, radio and recorded music, a through sleeper from New Orleans (off train 75 at Clovis), and, of course, the attention-grabbing Big Domes. There were also through sleepers from Chicago to Phoenix, Lubbock, Texas, and Los Angeles.

''Inaugural ceremonies at the Oakland station for the run eastward June 6 were both solemn and exciting,'' according to *The Santa Fe Magazine*. ''A huge crowd was on hand for the event which was to see christening of the train in a sacred ceremony never before performed publicly. . . .

''Hopi Chief Taptuka christened the San Francisco Chief with holy water collected in a private religious ceremony at San Francisco Peaks near Flagstaff, Arizona. . . . The 30-minute christening ceremonies are held to dedicate new Indian Kivas, official ceremonial chambers which are sacred to Indians. The activity in connection with the San Francisco Chief was the first time it had been presented to foreign eyes.''

Perhaps some charm was indeed imparted to the train, for it grew in the 1960's to be one of Santa Fe's longest consists. And it survived intact until the advent of Amtrak in 1971, while the *California Zephyr* died and the *City of San Francisco* was cut to triweekly.

In the summer of 1955 the train received its first additional blessing: a 4-drawing-room 1-double-bedroom lounge added to the consist. These cars were round-end observations from the original lightweight *Chief: Betahtakin, Biltabito, Chaistla, Chuska, Denehotso,* and *Puye*. They had been withdrawn from the *Chief* in the summer of 1954 and blunt-ended for mid-train operation in San Francisco service. In January of 1958, the *Vista*-series observations (which had been blunt-ended in 1956) were removed from the *Super Chief* and entered *San Francisco Chief* service, running along with *Denehotso* and *Puye*. The other Indian-named former observations went into storage.

In early 1954 when Santa Fe's Big Domes rolled out of Budd's Red Lion Plant into *El Cap* service, they seemed radically huge and innovative. But even then Budd and Santa Fe had something bigger and better coming down the line: ''Hi-Level'' cars, a totally new concept in long-distance rail travel and one that would remain uniquely Santa Fe until, two decades later, Amtrak embraced it in building its Superliner fleet.

Because the technology was so revolutionary, Santa Fe chose to order a pair of prototypes from Budd to operate for a trial period—much as it had back in 1936 with single-level prototype lightweight chair cars No. 3070 from Budd and No. 3071 from St. Louis Car Company. The two Hi-Levels—coaches 526 and 527—were unveiled in July 1954 and placed in the consist of *El Capitan* for testing. All the passenger seating was on the upper level, far from the noise and vibration of wheel on rail. Entries, restrooms, and luggage storage were on the lower level. With these functions removed, the upper level could comfortably seat sixty-seven passengers, compared to forty-four to forty-eight in single-level long-distance coaches. Air-

INVITATION TO PLEASURE When you board the Santa Fe's great new San Francisco Chief, you step into another world . . . a world of quiet and comfort, of beauty and exciting scenes, where sociability and serenity are your companions.

Featured among the San Francisco Chief's many stainless steel Budd cars are the spectacular "Big Domes" from which you can view the Santa Fe's magnificent and varied scenery as it has never been seen before while, if you wish, enjoying your favorite refreshments.

The San Francisco Chief is a wonderful example of the way the nation's railroads are making rail travel as enjoyable as it is dependable and safe. Never has the invitation to go by rail been so compelling.

The Budd Company, Philadelphia, Detroit, Gary.

Automobile, Trailer and Truck Bodies and Wheels, Railway Passenger Cars

PIONEERS IN BETTER TRANSPORTATION

conditioning units and other machinery were also on the lower level, where they could be serviced from aboard the train while it was in motion.

Pleased with these features, and seeing that the public was too, Santa Fe in 1955 ordered a fleet of Hi-Levels to re-equip *El Capitan;* twenty-five 72-passenger chair cars, ten 68-passenger chair cars (which, like the two prototypes, had stairs at one end leading down to connect with conventional single-level cars), six 88-passenger dome-type lounges, and six 80-seat diners. In addition, six baggage-dormitory cars—Nos. 3477-3482—were fitted with Hi-Level adapters (basically airfoils, but of more cosmetic than practical value) to become transition cars. Two of these, Nos. 3480 and 3481, had been delivered as baggage-dormitory-chair cars in 1938 for the original *El Cap,* providing a curious continuity in the otherwise unprecedented Hi-Level train.

The new equipment was virtually identical in design specifications to the two prototype cars. Passenger representatives had ridden aboard those experimental Hi-Levels, checking their performance and compiling data on customer reaction. They found little to change. On a typical September 1954 trip, for instance, seventy-three of seventy-nine passengers liked the new cars. A few missed small racks on the upper level for hats and parcels; in the production run, such racks were added. A more serious problem was the difficulty for the elderly or handicapped in going downstairs to use the restrooms. Santa Fe responded by adding bathrooms at one end of the lounge cars and reserving seats in the adjacent coach for passengers who found the stairs inconvenient.

Each of the new train's five consists would include seven coaches (expandable to nine in summer), one diner, and one lounge. With seven coaches, the passenger capacity was 496, compared to 350 for the eight-coach single-level consist being replaced. The Hi-Level cars stood fifteen and one-half feet, two feet taller than conventional cars, but their floors were eight feet above the rails, four feet higher than aboard single-level cars, providing a substantially better view and a much smoother and quieter ride. Passengers boarded the coaches through center doors at platform level, moving right in without vestibule steps to climb.

On the upper level of the chair cars, carpeting was a cactus leaf pattern in henna and turquoise. The wainscot was turquoise, and the window pier panels had a special silk-screen design on a background of frost walnut pickwood. The fully reclining seats, equipped with a new type of leg rest and upholstered in a turquoise needlepoint, had fifty-inch spacing between rows.

The diner's upper level accommodated eighty patrons per sitting at nineteen tables for four and two for two. (Santa Fe's conventional diners seated thirty-six and most of their lunch-counter diners thirty-three.) The decor was similar to the coaches': Zuni turquoise and frost walnut. The upholstery for the chairs was a coral red mohair, and the tables were a gray Formica adorned with a delicate pattern in lighter gray and pink. The 36-foot kitchen on the lower level was the largest ever on a train. From there, two elevators carried the food to the patrons on the upper level.

The "Top of the Cap," as the lounge car was called, seated sixty on the upper level in a variety of groupings: banquette sections for four, small tables for two, and single easy chairs, plus a few tables accommodating foursomes for bridge. Upholstery was Naugahyde in tones of coral, burnished antique beige, sandalwood, and turquoise. Wainscot and low partitions were turquoise, pier panels rose beige, and ceilings orchid gray. On the rear bulkhead was a large etched mirror—which was in fact a one-way mirror, allowing the attendant to keep tabs on the needs of his patrons from the galley behind. All the way to the rear, beyond the galley, was a newsstand selling magazines, souvenirs, stationery, and sundries.

In the Hi-Level *El Capitan* Santa Fe had something totally new to show off; therefore, the railroad made more of the exhibition tour and inaugural ceremonies than it had since the first streamlined *Super Chief* of 1937 entered service. For one thing, the train was exhibited in the East, not just at on-line cities. No doubt Santa Fe would have liked to display its new goods in New York City—where back in 1946, its Alco PA's had made a big hit under the Waldorf-Astoria—but clearances prohibited, so Washington became the destination instead.

Facing page: A Leslie Regan painting — one of an extensive series done for The Budd Company — illustrates a 1954 Budd ad from *National Geographic* featuring the *San Francisco Chief.* Above, Hi-Level coach No. 700. Right is an exploded view of the projected Hi-Level dining car configuration. SANTA FE RAILWAY.

Above, the Hi-Level *El Capitan* climbs Raton Pass; in the foreground is the dome-like lounge. Right, the cover from a brochure touting Hi-Level service on *El Cap.* (Some of the contents appear overleaf.) SANTA FE RAILWAY, ABOVE Facing page: The Hi-Level diner (top) and lounge (bottom). SANTA FE RAILWAY; DIAGRAM AT FAR RIGHT, ROBERT J. WAYNER COLLECTION

Floor Plans and Seating Arrangements of the New HI-LEVEL El Capitan

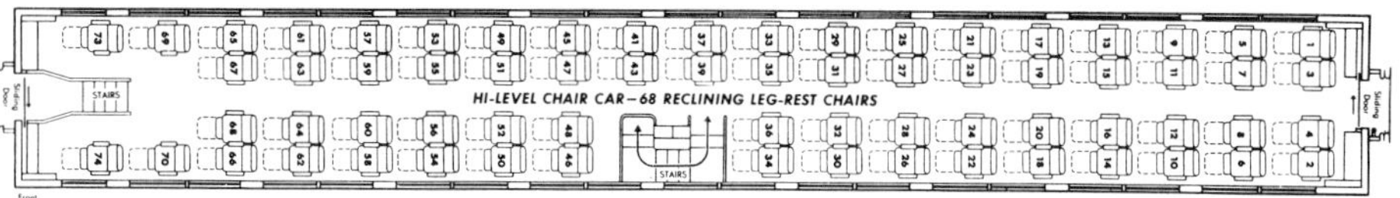

Seating arrangement of 68-Seat HI-LEVEL Chair Car with stairs at front end of car
(In consist of train this is Car No. 216-Westbound; Car No. 226-Eastbound)

Seating arrangement of 72-Seat HI-LEVEL Chair Car, no stairs at either end
(Car No. 215, 214, 213, 212, 211-Westbound; Car No. 225, 224, 223, 222, 221-Eastbound)

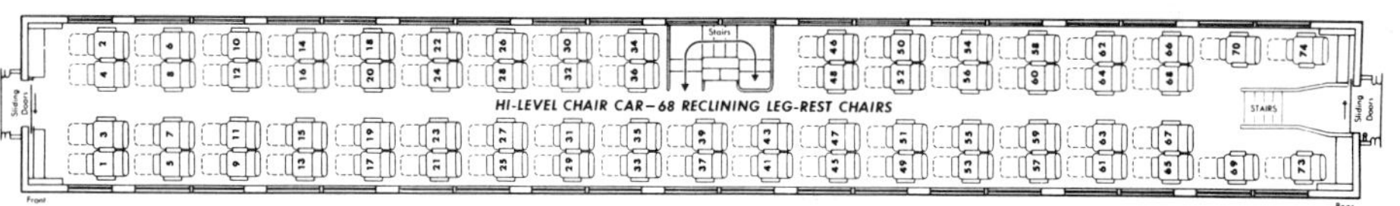

Seating arrangement of 68-Seat HI-LEVEL Chair Car with stairs at rear end of car
(In consist of train this Car No. 210-Westbound; Car No. 220-Eastbound)

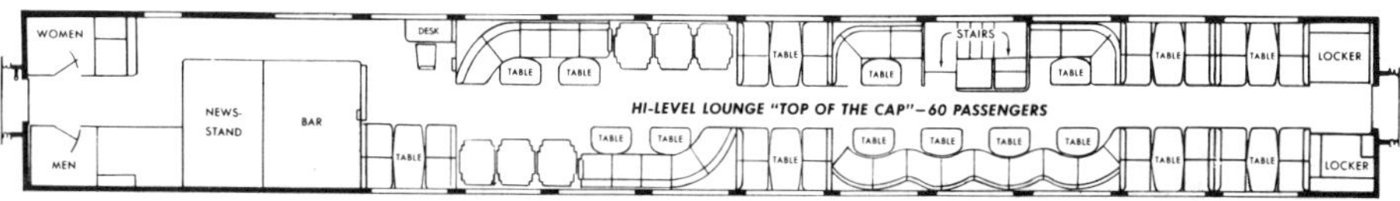

Floor plan of "TOP OF THE CAP"—HI-LEVEL El Capitan Lounge Car

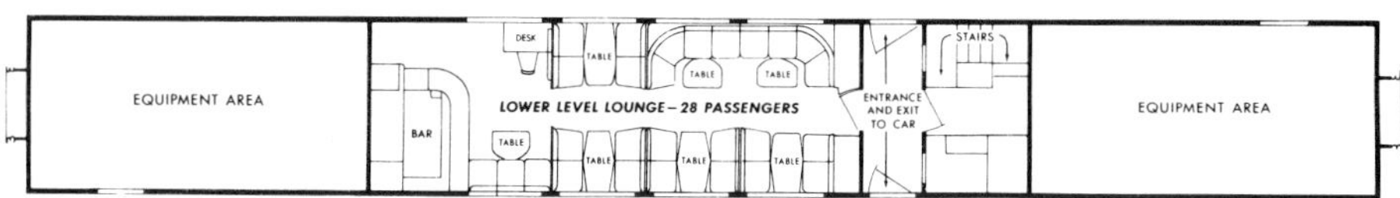

Floor plan of Lower Level Lounge of the HI-LEVEL El Capitan Lounge Car

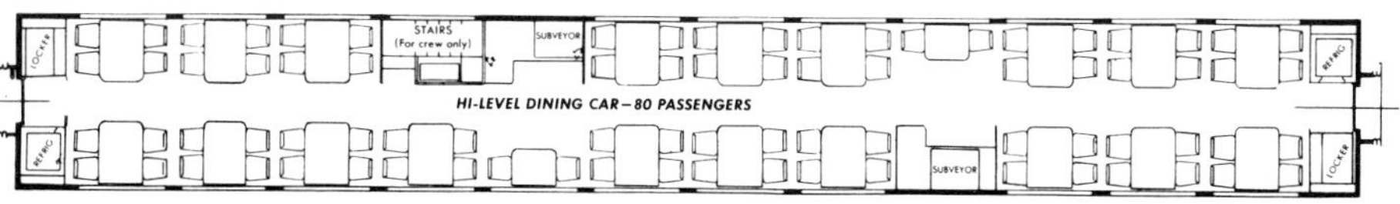

Floor plan of 80-Seat Dining Room—HI-LEVEL El Capitan

The Hi-Level's eastern odyssey began late in the evening of June 15, 1956, when Santa Fe turned the tall consist over to Baltimore & Ohio at that railroad's Lincoln Street Yard in Chicago for an overnight run to Pittsburgh. There, the next morning, the demonstration *El Cap* entrained 150 passengers—representatives from newspapers, magazines, radio, television, the Santa Fe, and The Budd Company—for the all-day run to Washington on the B&O, via Connellsville, Grafton, and Keyser.

At Washington, a second Hi-Level diner was added to the consist. This allowed the railroad to feed great numbers of guests on four two-and-one-half-hour excursions to Point of Rocks, Maryland, which it operated for lunch and dinner on June 18 and dinner the following two evenings. The guests, numbering as many as four hundred, were senators, congressmen, members of the Interstate Commerce Commission and various other government departments and agencies, and the press on the dinner trips; and invitees of the freight and passenger departments for the luncheon jaunt. All dined on Philadelphia pepper pot, roast tenderloin of beef with fresh mushroom sauce, and fresh strawberry shortcake with whipped cream.

While the cars were idle between meal trips, they were on display for the public at Washington's Eckington Yard. On June 18, only four cars were open and a special luncheon was held aboard the second diner. The next day nine cars were open, allowing two visiting lines.

Immediately after their return from the June 19 dinner outing to Point of Rocks, the cars headed west, back over the B&O to Pittsburgh, where they were exhibited the following day. However, a representative selection of cars from the consist was cut out and, in mid-afternoon, sent ahead to Youngstown for exhibition that evening. Afterward, those cars moved on to Cleveland for display the next day, while the cars remaining in Pittsburgh deadheaded back to Chicago. That was on June 21; on June 22 came another all-day exhibition, in Detroit, before return to Chicago.

There some cars went on exhibit for two days—June 23 and 24—while a sixteen-car consist (including two conventional diners) ran luncheon round trips to Streator, Illinois, for ticket agents from other railroads, encouragement to them to route through passengers on *El Capitan*. The next day an eleven-car train, with both available Hi-Level diners, ran a dinner trip to Streator and back for five hundred guests of the freight, passenger, tax, and legal departments. Meanwhile, enough equipment had been moved to Kansas

City for a 10 a.m.-4 p.m. exhibition at Union Terminal on June 26. That evening, a twelve-car consist took six hundred guests round-trip to Emporia, Kansas, with dinner en route. From there it was off to the West Coast for exhibitions at Los Angeles, Pasadena, San Bernardino, San Diego, and Long Beach.

All these comings and goings, showings and hostings, culminated July 8 in Albuquerque, when inaugural east- and westbound Hi-Level *El Capitans* (laden with railfans, on an outing promoted by *Trains* Magazine), met in front of the historic Santa Fe station and Alvarado Hotel for a christening ceremony, part of Albuquerque's 250th anniversary celebration. President Gurley presented the city with a retired steam locomotive for its Coronado Park. Mrs. Gurley, along with Mayor Maurice Sanchez's wife, christened the trains, breaking bottles of Great Lakes and Pacific Ocean water on the locomotive's noses.

The first arrival of a Santa Fe train in Alburquerque in 1880 was reenacted by a replica of Santa Fe locomotive No. 1, the *Cyrus K. Holliday,* pulling two old coaches of costumed townspeople. The Duke and Duchess of Alburquerque (the original spelling) in Spain were on hand, as was "Miss Hi-Level," Marcia Drewry. Two colorfully garbed actors posing as Spanish *conquistadores* handed out souvenirs. At 4:30 and 5:00 p.m., the inaugural Hi-Level *El Caps* resumed their journeys, Chicago and Los Angeles-bound. A week later, on July 15, regular Hi-Level service began.

The conventional cars thus replaced found their way into other trains. Most notably, the 506-series Big Domes and the coach-observations went to the *Chief.* The domes would remain for the rest of that train's career, the observations only briefly. Santa Fe had already grown negative about observation cars for the switching complications they presented; only an acute shortage of chair cars reprieved them at all. When, temporarily in the spring of 1957 and permanently at the end of that summer, the *Kansas Cityan* was discontinued east of Kansas City and its through cars carried to Chicago by the *Chief,* the observations disappeared.

Though the equipment headlines in the mid fifties clearly were grabbed by *El Capitan,* its all-Pullman running mate was not ignored. In 1957 and '58, the *Super Chief*'s feature cars were redecorated. The Pleasure Dome's main lounge received new furniture and a lowered ceiling, incorporating indirect lighting and a multi-vent air distribution system. Walls were covered in smoky gray vinyl, window draperies were gold and white, and the thick carpeting was charcoal-colored.

In the Santa Fe tradition of decorating with Indian art were a pair of sand paintings flanking the door into the car. Entitled "Indian Chant," they were done by Luther A. Douglas, using sand from every state served by the railroad. A third sand painting by Douglas adorned the under-dome cocktail lounge, cozy with soft gray-and-yellow striped carpeting, mocha drapes, and diffused light from three columnar brass and copper lamps. The Turquoise Room and dome area were also completely redecorated, as were the diners and dormitory-lounge cars—the latter receiving the furniture removed from the Pleasure Domes' lounges. All the cars were equipped with outside swing-hanger trucks for a better ride.

But the biggest news in 1958 regarding the *Super Chief* wasn't cosmetic but operational. On January 12, that premier train was combined with *El Capitan*, effectively ending all-Pullman service on Santa Fe. (Though the consists were split in peak seasons for the next decade, except for the short Christmas rush the *Super Chief* section would generally include some single-level coaches.)

This move had more symbolic than practical impact. The two trains, though coupled together, continued to carry their traditional diners and lounges and retained their own identities. But the consolidation characterized the direction passenger service on Santa Fe would take from then on: an attempt to maintain quality while holding costs in line and trimming services to reflect diminished demand.

Left, a shining *El Cap* rolls through the agricultural countryside of southern California. The "transition car" — a baggage-dormitory equipped with airfoil adapter — is well displayed in this view. Top right, *El Capitan*'s courier-nurses, wearing uniforms of turquoise and mesa blue, pose in the doorway of a Hi-Level coach. Bottom right, for decades — and still in 1986 — a fork-lift-mounted washer scrubbed windows at Albuquerque. SANTA FE RAILWAY, LEFT AND TOP RIGHT; STEVE PATTERSON, BOTTOM RIGHT

Top left, the Hi-Level *El Capitan* climbs Raton Pass, near where the old Wootton Toll Road, part of the Santa Fe Trail, cut through the mountains; Fisher's Peak at the left is a prominent landmark. Top right, again on Raton Pass, the eastbound *Chief* — now carrying a Big Dome that had belonged to *El Cap* briefly before the advent of the Hi-Levels — has just left the city of Raton, New Mexico. Left, though the Hi-Level *El Capitan* of course never had an observation car, it did carry a drumhead, as here on August 6, 1962, awaiting departure from Los Angeles. SANTA FE RAILWAY, TOP; STAN KISTLER, LEFT

7

Meals by Fred Harvey

Left, *Super Chief* chef Herman Sirio carves a turkey in the dining car's compact kitchen. Right, a couple offers a toast to the camera in the post-1957 Turquoise Room, keynoted as in the original decor by a shadow-boxed turquoise medallion. "Santa Fe" marking is clearly visible on the frosty silver champagne bucket. China is Mimbreno. SANTA FE RAILWAY

Dinner in the diner was always a special and renowned experience aboard the *Super Chief* and the Santa Fe's other streamliners, a highlight of any trip. This tradition of exellence in railroad dining went back well beyond the lightweight era and, in fact, even beyond dining cars. It was embodied in the phrase "Meals by Fred Harvey," which began for Santa Fe passengers in 1876.

Railroad dining has not always been pleasant or elegant. Santa Fe began operating passenger trains in the early 1870's; in those days, for travelers aboard any railroad's trains, there was eating to stave off hunger, not dining for pleasure. Dining cars were virtually nonexistent. (George M. Pullman's *Delmonico,* generally considered the first true dining car, was built in 1868, but years passed before the idea caught on in any substantial way.) Meals were generally taken at hasty stops, where passengers were often overcharged and underserved by a management secure in the knowledge that its clientele would within moments be headed out of town aboard a train, most likely never to return. Into this dismal situation came a man destined to have a substantial impact on the second wave of settlement in the West—an impact truly unique for a hotelier and restaurateur.

That man was Frederick Henry Harvey, and his biography could read like this: Born June 27, 1835, of Scottish and English parents, he came to the United States in 1850, a fifteen-year-old on a sailing ship amid an army of immigrants. His first job in New York City, his port of debarkation, was as a dishwasher, at $2 a week. Harvey saved money for boat passage to New Orleans, where he found work in some of the finest restaurants and hotels. This immersion in a world of elegant dining presumably planted the seed that many years later would flower into Harvey Houses. After four years of work in St. Louis as a tailor and jeweler he had the funds to open a restaurant with a partner—who soon absconded with the substantial proceeds of the venture.

Again at loose ends, Harvey, by then married to Barbara Sarah Mattos, moved obliquely toward railroading—via work with the Missouri River Packet Line and, later, the St. Joseph Post Office, sorting mail on the first RPO. Recognizing that railroads were in their ascendency, he hired on with the Hannibal & St. Joseph and then the Chicago, Burlington & Quincy, as freight agent in Leavenworth, Kansas.

The peripatetic Harvey's simultaneous interests also included a ranch which he had purchased, a hotel in

Hutchinson, Kansas, Harvey Girls of 1926, posing on the porch of the dining room (top) and inside, with customers (bottom). Facing page: The facade of El Navajo at Gallup, New Mexico, and a lunch counter with a lone Harvey Girl in attendance. SANTA FE RAILWAY, BOTH PAGES

which he'd invested, and the Leavenworth *Times and Conservative*, for which he sold advertising. These pursuits took him into the hinterlands, where he was appalled by the poor quality of the restaurant service. At railroad meal stops, the food was unappetizing—but patrons often were unable to eat it anyway, since trainmen colluded with the restaurants, agreeing for a price to blow the whistle for departure before the customers had had the alloted time to eat their food, which thus was left behind and could be served again.

Fred Harvey saw a market for good food, well served and reasonably priced. He first approached Burlington officials with this thought. Though they did not disagree with his premise, they were not interested in getting involved in the restaurant business. As a result, Harvey went to Santa Fe superintendent Charles F. Morse, who *was* interested. From the gentlemen's agreement they reached came an extraordinary empire of Santa Fe-owned, Fred Harvey-operated restaurants, hotels, and dining cars.

The first was the lunchroom in the Santa Fe depot in Topeka, Kansas, which Harvey took over in 1876. Ground rules laid from the beginning were to last, in spirit, for the better part of a century: AT&SF would supply without charge the buildings, coal, ice, water, and transportation for Harvey's furnishings, food, supplies, and personnel. All profits would go to Fred Harvey. The benefit to the Santa Fe would be attractive dining service for its customers.

As the Harvey empire evolved, the railroad's gains from this partnership became even more substantial. Moving on from the Topeka lunchroom to a hotel in Florence, Kansas, bought by the Santa Fe and renovated by Fred and Sarah Harvey, the enterprise grew to encompass lunchrooms lined up all along the Santa Fe route to California at roughly one-hundred-mile intervals and a chain of fine hotels, many at tourist destinations. These didn't just serve Santa Fe's existing customers but actually generated new businerss for the railroad, being attractions in themselves.

In style and ambiance, the hotels reflected Southwestern culture, both Indian and Spanish, as their names suggested: El Ortiz, Alvarado, El Navajo, La Fonda, La Posada, El Tovar. For many of these, interiors (and in some cases exteriors) were designed by

Mary Colter, the Fred Harvey-Santa Fe architect and designer who created the famous Minbreno china for the *Super Chief,* and that train's silverware as well. (A Colter specialty was individualization. The Minbreno china featured thirty-seven unique designs, each piece different. For La Fonda, the hotel in Santa Fe, New Mexico, Colter designed 156 guest rooms, no two alike.)

But Harvey Houses were perhaps most famous for serving train passengers at meal stops, and the key to this well-orchestrated operation was the army of Harvey Girls who waited on table. These young women—"of good character, attractive and intelligent, ages 18-30," according to the newspaper ads that recruited them for $17.59 a month, plus tips—became an institution. They were pretty, industrious, efficient, and respectable, in a time and place—the still raw American West— when these characteristics were in short supply. Many Harvey Girls married Santa Fe railroaders and had an important stabilizing influence in a boisterous time. Estimates say that Fred Harvey brought more than five thousand girls West, most of whom married and stayed.

Decked out in plain black and white uniforms designed to mute their natural attractions, the girls presented a prim appearance. Most lived in dormitories with stern matrons in charge to see that their behavior was prim, too. But there was no disputing their attractiveness—nor their efficiency, both major factors in the success of the Harvey Houses. One often cited example of this efficiency was the "cup code"; after asking the patron his beverage preference, the waitress would communicate the response to the "drink girl" who followed her by adjusting the coffee cup—right side up for coffee, upside down for hot tea, upside down and tilted against the saucer for iced tea, upside down and off the saucer for milk.

This procedure is among the lore embodied in "The Harvey Girls," MGM's technicolor film of 1945 which starred Judy Garland and included Angela Lansbury, Ray Bolger, and Cyd Charisse in the cast. Most memorable from Harry Warren and Johnny Mercer's score is the wonderfully bouncy "On the Atchison, Topeka, and the Santa Fe." Harvey Girls have a prominent place in American history, and this movie further popularized their role in bringing eastern civilization to the Wild West.

When dining cars came to the Santa Fe—in 1888, a full twenty years after the pioneering *Delmonico*'s introduction—Fred Harvey was given the responsibility of managing them. His reputation for excellence was already made. Eighty years of dining-car operation would do nothing but enhance it.

The first diners were carried by the *California Limited,* and to them Harvey brought the amenities of his fine restaurants. Linens were Irish, imported from John S. Brown and Sons, Belfast; silver was elegant and ornate. The menu was impressive, including littleneck clams on the half shell, filet mignon, broiled plover on toast, and strawberries and cream. Seventy-five cents bought such a feast.

It was still relatively early in the dining-car era when Fred Harvey died, in 1901, at the age of sixty-eight. At that time, his company's cooperative venture with the Santa Fe encompassed fifteen hotels, forty-seven restaurants, and thirty dining cars, plus the food service on the San Francisco Bay ferry system. Fred's sons Ford and Byron were already deeply involved in management; under their direction the Fred Harvey

Dining-car development through the years, from turn-of-the-century opulence (right), through a simpler but still elegant *Scout* heavyweight (below), through an early *Chief* lightweight (far right), to the *Super Chief* diners that ended passenger service on the Santa Fe (facing page).
SANTA FE RAILWAY

Company would sustain the excellence begun by their father. In their era the great resort hotels—most notably El Tovar, at Grand Canyon—were built and the dining-car fleet expanded.

Half a century later, in 1954, the Fred Harvey Company and Santa Fe operated 122 dining cars, staffed by more than two thousand stewards, chefs, waiters, cooks, and buffet attendants. All these men reported then to R. T. Hillyard, superintendent of dining cars, who reported to Harold R. Ray, head of the dining car department, who reported to Byron Harvey, Jr., president of the Fred Harvey Company.

The dining-car department which these men supervised was a large and complex organization, with many experts employed both on-board and off. First the food had to be purchased, and this was done by career professionals who were specialists. The finest meats were chosen directly from packing houses in Chicago and Los Angeles; once selected and stamped "Fred Harvey," steer carcasses were hung on hooks to age for two weeks. Fresh fruits or vegetables might have come from the West Coast or from Chicago's South Water Market, depending on the season. (Two refrigerator cars shuttled back and forth weekly so that particular fresh foods could be available at both starting points.) Fresh fish came from all over: oysters, lobsters, and clams from the Atlantic; whitefish from

Lake Superior; shrimp from the Gulf of Mexico; and trout (a particular favorite through the years, ordered by 33,811 patrons even in mid-Depression 1933, for instance) from the Rocky Mountains.

The main commissary was at Chicago; there chefs carried on experimental cooking and recipe development. Cooks prepared soups and sauce stocks and made meats oven ready—except steaks, which were cut to order on the diners. Bakers prepared pies, cakes, cookies, and pastries, including Santa Fe's famous Dobos tortes. Other commissaries were located in California at Oakland, Bakersfield, and Los Angeles; at Clovis, New Mexico; at Kansas City; and at Houston. And there were additional supply stations where stocks could be replenished and perishable items picked up. At La Junta, Colorado, for instance, westbound trains took aboard fresh trout.

There were laundries at San Bernadino, California, Albuquerque, New Mexico, and Newton, Kansas, where waiters' uniforms and table linen were made snowy and starched. Also at Newton, the Fred Harvey Company had a bottling plant for dairy products and soft drinks.

All these dimensions to Santa Fe dining-car service were behind the scenes, invisible to the patron and thus but dimly appreciated. Much more in the limelight was what actually went on aboard the 122 dining cars. It

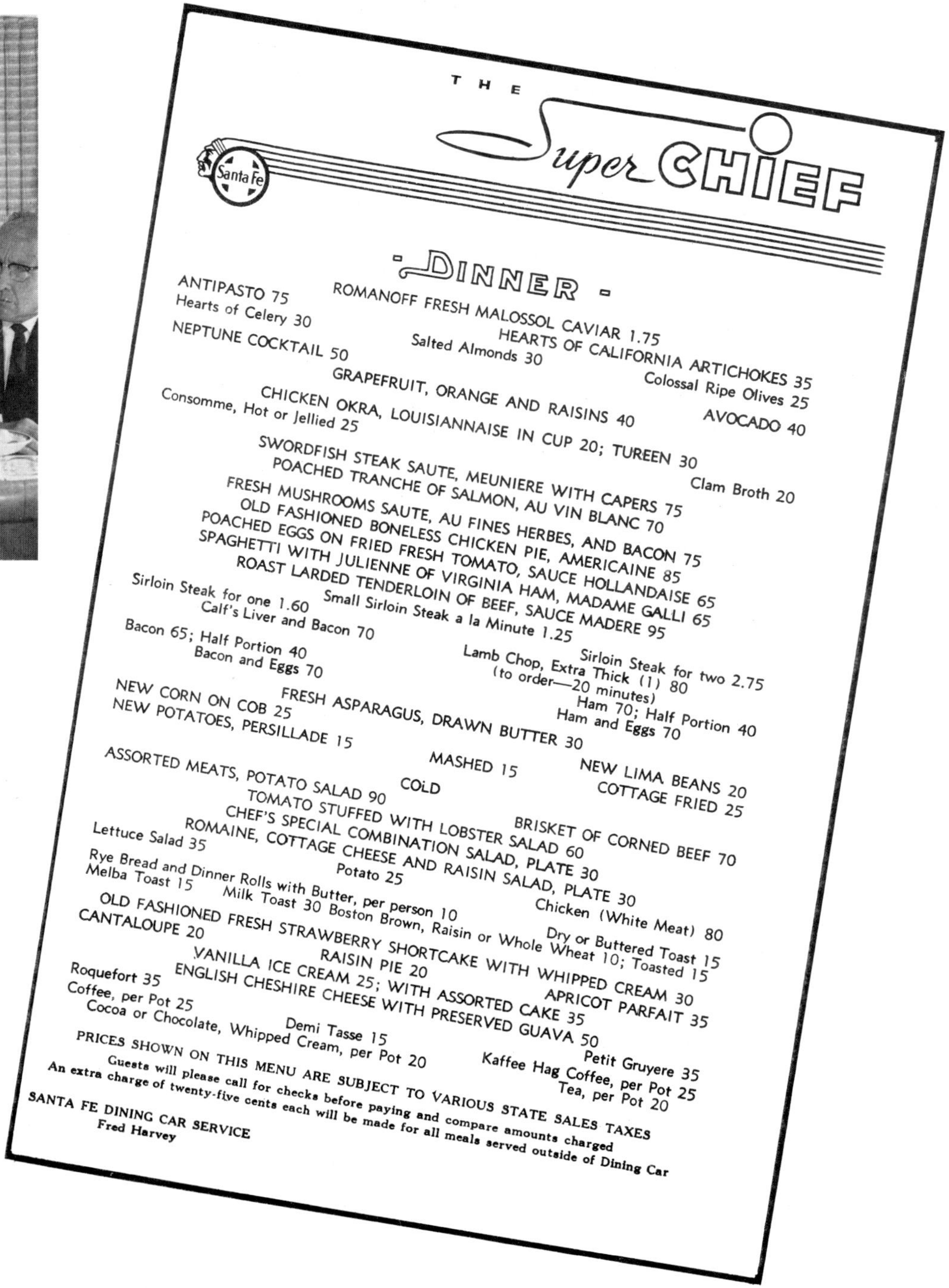

THE Super CHIEF

Santa Fe

DINNER

ANTIPASTO 75 / ROMANOFF FRESH MALOSSOL CAVIAR 1.75
Hearts of Celery 30 / HEARTS OF CALIFORNIA ARTICHOKES 35
NEPTUNE COCKTAIL 50 / Salted Almonds 30 / Colossal Ripe Olives 25
GRAPEFRUIT, ORANGE AND RAISINS 40 / AVOCADO 40
Consomme, Hot or Jellied 25 / CHICKEN OKRA, LOUISIANNAISE IN CUP 20; TUREEN 30 / Clam Broth 20
SWORDFISH STEAK SAUTE, MEUNIERE WITH CAPERS 75
POACHED TRANCHE OF SALMON, AU VIN BLANC 70
FRESH MUSHROOMS SAUTE, AU FINES HERBES, AND BACON 75
OLD FASHIONED BONELESS CHICKEN PIE, AMERICAINE 85
POACHED EGGS ON FRIED FRESH TOMATO, SAUCE HOLLANDAISE 65
SPAGHETTI WITH JULIENNE OF VIRGINIA HAM, MADAME GALLI 65
ROAST LARDED TENDERLOIN OF BEEF, SAUCE MADERE 95
Sirloin Steak for one 1.60 / Small Sirloin Steak a la Minute 1.25 / Sirloin Steak for two 2.75
Calf's Liver and Bacon 70 / Lamb Chop, Extra Thick (1) 80 (to order—20 minutes)
Bacon 65; Half Portion 40 / Ham 70; Half Portion 40
Bacon and Eggs 70 / Ham and Eggs 70
NEW CORN ON COB 25 / FRESH ASPARAGUS, DRAWN BUTTER 30
NEW POTATOES, PERSILLADE 15 / MASHED 15 / NEW LIMA BEANS 20
COTTAGE FRIED 25
ASSORTED MEATS, POTATO SALAD 90 / COLD / BRISKET OF CORNED BEEF 70
TOMATO STUFFED WITH LOBSTER SALAD 60
CHEF'S SPECIAL COMBINATION SALAD, PLATE 30
ROMAINE, COTTAGE CHEESE AND RAISIN SALAD, PLATE 30
Lettuce Salad 35 / Potato 25 / Chicken (White Meat) 80
Rye Bread and Dinner Rolls with Butter, per person 10
Melba Toast 15 / Milk Toast 30 / Boston Brown, Raisin or Whole Wheat 10; Toasted 15 / Dry or Buttered Toast 15
OLD FASHIONED FRESH STRAWBERRY SHORTCAKE WITH WHIPPED CREAM 30
CANTALOUPE 20 / RAISIN PIE 20 / APRICOT PARFAIT 35
VANILLA ICE CREAM 25; WITH ASSORTED CAKE 35
Roquefort 35 / ENGLISH CHESHIRE CHEESE WITH PRESERVED GUAVA 50 / Petit Gruyere 35
Coffee, per Pot 25 / Demi Tasse 15 / Kaffee Hag Coffee, per Pot 25
Cocoa or Chocolate, Whipped Cream, per Pot 20 / Tea, per Pot 20

PRICES SHOWN ON THIS MENU ARE SUBJECT TO VARIOUS STATE SALES TAXES

Guests will please call for checks before paying and compare amounts charged

An extra charge of twenty-five cents each will be made for all meals served outside of Dining Car

SANTA FE DINING CAR SERVICE
Fred Harvey

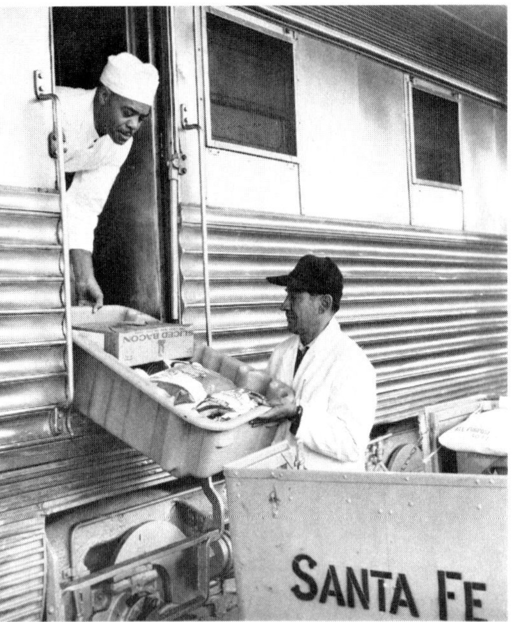

Much went on behind the scenes before a Fred Harvey meal was placed in front of a dining-car patron. Butchers prepared meat in the commissaries (top left); dining cars had to be provisioned, as here at Los Angeles (top right); and the food cooked aboard to order (right). Then it was elegantly served (facing page). SANTA FE RAILWAY, ALL PHOTOS; MENU, PETER TILP COLLECTION

took an average of 114 regularly assigned crews to man these cars—with as many as thirty-five more called on to meet the demands of the peak summer season. A standard diner had a crew of eleven: steward; chef; second, third, and fourth cooks; and six waiters.

Each of these eleven had very specific duties. The steward's was the most obvious and most visible: greet and seat customers, issue menus and meal checks, offer suggestions, handle money, and generally oversee service aboard his car. The division of responsibilities for the other ten was far less obvious. The following description, from the September 1954 *Santa Fe Magazine*, shows how remarkably well orchestrated and complex dining car procedures were:

"The head cook in the dining car kitchen, as the name indicates, is the chef. He is an expert in his profession, having received his training in better hotels and restaurants in this country or abroad, or having served his apprenticeship aboard the cars.

"If the latter, he probably started as fourth cook, washed dishes and did other chores. When he became a third cook, he prepared breakfast dishes and other simple orders. Showing ability, he was promoted and transferred, now as a second cook, to work with a chef famed for his culinary skills. As other promotions follow, our cook, now experienced, may become a chef, at first on a train where traffic is not too heavy. Then, if he has exceptional ability, he may eventually become chef on the *Chief* or *Super Chief*.

"A waiter, in order to qualify for dining-car service, is required to have had experience in food service in better restaurants or hotels. Before taking his place aboard the dining car, he receives a thorough briefing. He then starts as sixth waiter in a crew of veterans who watch over him and gradually give him more and more responsibility as he proves his ability.

"In addition to serving meals, each waiter has side work to attend to such as, in part:

"Waiter No. 1 is the pantryman and tends to such work as the making of salads, desserts, dressings and cocktail sauces, according to the menu, and to keeping the pantry and ice boxes clean.

"Waiter No. 2 is the 'small silver man.' He cleans and polishes all silver before train departure and again after each meal.

"Waiter No. 3 has charge of all linen, salt and pepper shakers, sugar bowls and water bottles. Salt and pepper containers and sugar bowls are emptied and cleaned every day.

"Waiter No. 4 keeps fruit lockers clean and prepares all fresh fruit. He has charge of service trays and steel knives, jelly and jam containers. He also assists in receiving supplies aboard the train.

"Waiter No. 5 has charge of the ice cream supplies and sees to the cleaning of glasses and the large silver such as coffee pots and bowls. He also assists with supplies and ice.

"Waiter No. 6 assists the pantryman, and is a general handy man."

Encouraging each member of the crew, from the steward on down, to do his job well were eight traveling supervisors who rode the Santa Fe systemwide, keeping tabs on the level of dining-car service. These supervisors had been chefs or stewards themselves, so their suggestions—often in the form of written "reminders"—carried the weight of experience.

In the mid-fifties, Santa Fe operated six different types of food-service cars. There were the "straight" or conventional dining cars and lunch-counter diners common on the streamliners; cafe-observations ran on the *Centennial State* and *Oil Flyer;* and cafe-lounge cars on the *Tulsan*. In addition there were two innovations, both offered somewhat tentatively and with ample solicitation of customer comment: El Cafeteria and the Lunch-O-Mat.

In 1954 notices appeared aboard certain services to this effect: "On this train for a trial run is a new car, *El Cafeteria,* one of the latest innovations in railroad meal service.

"In this car you will be able to choose from a fine selection of food, eat what you please, and pay only for what you want. And the prices you pay for meals are the most economical offered on dining cars of any railroad.

"The food is the same as that carried on regular dining cars, but the service is designed to allow you to select your meals and serve yourself. . . .

"You are among the first travelers to use this service and we are anxious to know your reactions. After you have tried this unique service tell the steward in charge of *El Cafeteria* how it appeals to you."

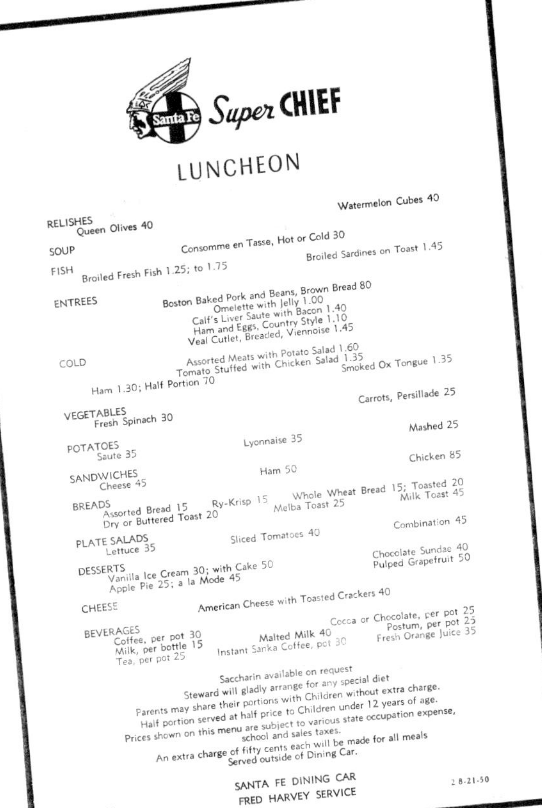

Santa Fe Super CHIEF

LUNCHEON

RELISHES
Queen Olives 40 — Watermelon Cubes 40

SOUP
Consomme en Tasse, Hot or Cold 30

FISH
Broiled Fresh Fish 1.25; to 1.75 — Broiled Sardines on Toast 1.45

ENTREES
Boston Baked Pork and Beans, Brown Bread 80
Omelette with Jelly 1.00
Calf's Liver Saute with Bacon 1.40
Ham and Eggs, Country Style 1.10
Veal Cutlet, Breaded, Viennoise 1.45

COLD
Assorted Meats with Potato Salad 1.60
Tomato Stuffed with Chicken Salad 1.35
Smoked Ox Tongue 1.35
Ham 1.30; Half Portion 70

VEGETABLES
Fresh Spinach 30 — Carrots, Persillade 25

POTATOES
Saute 35 — Lyonnaise 35 — Mashed 25

SANDWICHES
Cheese 45 — Ham 50 — Chicken 85

BREADS
Assorted Bread 15 — Ry-Krisp 15 — Whole Wheat Bread 15; Toasted 20
Dry or Buttered Toast 20 — Melba Toast 25 — Milk Toast 45

PLATE SALADS
Lettuce 35 — Sliced Tomatoes 40 — Combination 45

DESSERTS
Vanilla Ice Cream 30; with Cake 50 — Chocolate Sundae 40
Apple Pie 25; a la Mode 45 — Pulped Grapefruit 50

CHEESE
American Cheese with Toasted Crackers 40

BEVERAGES
Coffee, per pot 30 — Malted Milk 40 — Cocoa or Chocolate, per pot 25
Milk, per bottle 15 — Instant Sanka Coffee, pot 30 — Postum, per pot 25
Tea, per pot 25 — Fresh Orange Juice 35

Saccharin available on request
Steward will gladly arrange for any special diet
Parents may share their portions with Children without extra charge.
Half portion served at half price to Children under 12 years of age.
Prices shown on this menu are subject to various state occupation expense, school and sales taxes.
An extra charge of fifty cents each will be made for all meals Served outside of Dining Car.

SANTA FE DINING CAR
FRED HARVEY SERVICE

CSC — 2 8-21-50

Though designed to cut labor costs, these cafeteria cars were not totally dehumanized; an attendant was available to carry trays for children or the elderly. But the final step in reduction in personnel was taken in the Lunch-O-Mat, its name as inelegant as its ambiance. Aboard this converted coach, fully automatic, self-service, coin-operated machinery dispensed two varieties of radar-grilled hot sandwiches, two cold sandwiches, coffee, juices, milk, and pastry, all provided by Fred Harvey. No attendant was required aboard the Lunch-O-Mat, which was used exclusively on the El Paso, Texas-Albuquerque *El Pasoan*.

The Lunch-O-Mat, like El Cafeteria, was introduced in 1954. A few years earlier, in 1950, another deviation from the norm of full dining service had been instituted by Santa Fe: the re-establishment of dining station meal stops west of La Junta, Colorado, for the once-mighty *California Limited,* Nos. 3 and 4. This was a full-circle return to the lunchroom service that

first made Fred Harvey famous in the days of the Harvey Girls. Westbound, breakfast was served at the Alvarado Hotel in Albuquerque; lunch at El Navajo in Gallup, New Mexico; and dinner at the Fray Marcos in Williams, Arizona. Eastbound, breakfast was at the station dining room at Seligman, Arizona; lunch at La Posada Hotel at Winslow, Arizona; and dinner at the Alvarado. Typical table d'hote menus included a full breakfast featuring shirred eggs and bacon, $1.15; lunch of braised beef with noodles, $1.45; and roast turkey dinner with all the trimmings, $1.65.

But lunchroom stops and El Cafeteria and Lunch-O-Mat were the exceptions that proved the rule, and the rule aboard the *Chief* fleet was superb dining—in the 1950's as for many decades previous and one still to come. At the pinnacle was the *Super Chief,* offering cuisine as fine as any on wheels in the world. Aboard the *Chief*—as of January 1954, no longer all-Pullman—could be found a standard 36-seat diner and a lunch-counter diner. In summer, *El Capitan* sometimes ran in

The *Super*'s Champagne Dinner was Santa Fe's final effort at innovative elegance, originally priced at $6.50 in 1963; this menu from 1969 shows modest inflation.

two sections, carrying a total of 760 pasengers. Each section included two lunch-counter diners.

Though food in Fred Harvey's diners was consistently good through the decades, it changed as tastes changed, moving in the direction of simplicity. Earliest dinner menus from the *Super Chief* featured Romanoff Fresh Malossol Caviar; Chicken Okra, Louisiannaise, in either cup or tureen; and entrees such as Swordfish Steak Saute, Meuniere with Capers; Poached Tranche of Salmon, au Vin Blanc; Fresh Mushrooms Saute, au Fines Herbes, and Bacon; or Roast Larded Tenderloin of Beef, Sauce Madere. Breakfast was remarkably hearty: an entire section, three times as long as "cereals," was devoted to "steaks, chops, etc." and included chicken, calf's liver and bacon, and veal cutlet.

Though less grand and extensive, the early menus for the coach streamliners were far from unattractive. Boiled Chinook Salmon with Egg Sauce and Charcoal Broiled Sirloin Steak, Maitre d'Hotel, were among the dinner offerings in the *San Diegan*'s lunch-counter diner. In the *Chicagoan/Kansas Cityan*'s full diner table d'hote luncheons included Baked Fresh Mackerel, Creole; Ragout of Beef Tenderloin Tips with Fresh Vegetables; Baked Shoulder of Lamb with Onions and Potatoes, Boulangere Chicken Croquettes, Sauce Supreme; and Omlette with Shredded Ham, Currant Jelly.

In its first stainless-steel year, the *Chief* featured menus no less grand than the *Super*'s, offering Cream of Chicken a la Reine; Grilled Lake Superior Whitefish; Fillet Mignon Grilled, Fresh Button Mushrooms, aux Fines Herbes; and Roast Wisconsin Duckling, Green Apple Sauce. Table d'hote dinner cost $1.50; aboard the heavyweight *California Limited* of that period, a fine dinner could be had for $1.35.

The forties and even fifties brought relatively little change in menu. Caviar was of course long gone, and charcoal broiled steaks and chops—always a dining-car specialty—were becoming increasingly central, but in 1953 the *Chief*'s menu still offered Fresh Shrimp a la Newburg and, among the soups, Pot Au Feu, Henry IV, which certainly sounded impressive. The following year's *San Francisco Chief*'s menu included Fresh Shrimp Cocktail and Grilled Lake Superior Whitefish, Maitre d'Hotel, as well as the predictable prime ribs, breast of Chicken, and lamb chops.

Dining-car breakfasts were traditionally good, and Fred Harvey's were certainly no exception. All the expected fruits and juices were there (the orange juice fresh-squeezed aboard the better trains in the better times), as well as cereals, breads, bacon, ham, potatoes, and eggs: boiled, fried, shirred, scrambled, poached, or as an omelette—plain, Spanish, or mushroom. And there were pancakes.

But the breakfast item that became most famous was the fat, tasty, railroad-style French toast. In 1960 Santa Fe served close to a million breakfasts in its dining cars, and French toast was the most popular item. This puffy, golden brown delicacy had been part of Santa Fe breakfasts since 1918 and had been a perennial favorite with travelers. The secret to success was placing the fried slice of bread in a 400-degree oven for a few minutes to cause it to puff, giving it the crispness that made it special.

The last important innovation in Santa Fe meal service came with the introduction on May 1, 1963, of the Champagne Dinner aboard the *Super Chief*. For $6.50, this table d'hote dinner included complimentary champagne or sparkling burgundy, appetizer, soup, entree, baked or french fried potato, tossed green salad, rolls, dessert, coffee, and after-dinner mints. The entrees: "A King-Size Cut of Succulent Roast Prime Ribs of Beef wth Fresh Horseradish Sauce Served as you like it—Rare, Medium, or Well Done," broiled African lobster tails, breast of chicken, or London mixed grill. At the same time this luxurious option was added for *Super Chief* customers, meal coupon books at reduced prices were available for travel aboard the *Chief*, *San Francisco Chief*, and *El Capitan*. In addition, *El Cap* offered an early "Chico Meal"—a full-course dinner for just $1.95.

From the early days of Santa Fe dining cars, the notation "Fred Harvey Service" always appeared at the bottom of menus, a hallmark of quality. But as the sixties wore on, the Fred Harvey name grew obscure and remote aboard the diners. No longer was the once-telling phrase prominent on the menu. In fact, The Fred Harvey Company had been sold to Amfac, though the Harvey name was retained. As Santa Fe passenger service diminished, management felt the Fred Harvey participation—far from what it used to be anyway—had become too expensive to justify. Accordingly, on January 1, 1969, the Santa Fe-Fred Harvey alliance was severed—ending a period of fruitful cooperation that had stretched over ninety-three years.

But even then the style and excellence that had been associated with Fred Harvey didn't die. To the end of Santa Fe operation the *Super Chief* menu offered Colorado Mountain Trout, Saute Almondine; Charcoal Broiled French Lamb Chops, General Grant; and Charcoal Broiled Filet Mignon on Crouton, Sauce Bearnaise. The cream of mushroom soup, aux croutons, or chicken gumbo were still available either by cup or by tureen—the tureen still handsome, ornate silver and the cup Mimbreno china. The ghost of Fred Harvey could rest peacefully, at least for a while.

Left, the Lunch-O-Mat car, at this time in service on the Richmond-Bakersfield *Golden Gate,* did not represent one of Fred Harvey's finest moments. Much better was the famous French toast, served here on "California Poppy" china (right). SANTA FE RAILWAY

SANTA FE

8

The Passing of the Chiefs

On October 5, 1965, the eastbound *Chief* is on Raton Pass, still an impressive train with five "Warbonnetted" F's and a Big Dome lounge, though it would not live through the decade. VICTOR HAND

Santa Fe and its most direct competitor, Union Pacific, were of all American railroads perhaps the two most tenaciously committed to passenger trains in the dark decade before Amtrak. While other lines, particularly those in the East but notably the Southern Pacific as well, headed early in the direction of pessimism, retrenchment, train-offs, deferred maintenance, and reduction of amenities, AT&SF kept making noises of qualified optimism and, into the mid-sixties, even ordered new equipment and rebuilt obsolete cars on hand. Appropriately, Santa Fe and UP, fierce competitors throughout the streamlined era, remained so until the end.

But in volume, the Santa Fe was in a class by itself, in 1966 operating 14 million train miles, compared to 8.4 million for Union Pacific, 7.8 million for Burlington, and 6.3 million for Southern Pacific. For the Santa Fe, this figure was down 30 percent from 19.9 million in 1957. (For Espee, the drop was closer to 50 percent over the same period.) Santa Fe remained positive, perhaps unrealistically so, but did effect economies that would not unacceptably compromise service standards.

The *Super/El Cap* consolidation was the most visible. In announcing the change, R. T. Anderson, Santa Fe's general traffic manager, said that the *Super Chief* could handle ninety to one hundred passengers but had gone out with as few as nineteen, and that *El Cap*, equipped for four hundred-plus, carried fewer than half that number at times. By combining the trains during the light travel times—October and November, and January 15 through April 30—the railroad hoped to save half a million dollars a month.

Other changes to the *Super Chief* consist occurred simultaneously with the consolidation. The *Vista*-series observations, which had been blunt-ended in 1956, were transferred to the *San Francisco Chief;* two of the three transcontinental sleeping cars were discontinued; and the mid-train dormitory lounges went into storage until the trains were split again for the summer season.

Additional prunings to other services came in 1958. No. 10, the eastbound *Kansas City Chief,* was discontinued east of Kansas City in the spring; its cars were given to the *Chief.* In September, No. 61, one of the four *Golden Gate* schedules, left the timecard. (The other three, Nos. 60, 62, and 63, survived until April 1965.) Other casualties were the *Golden Gate*'s coach-observations. In fact, in short order all the Budd coach- and parlor-observations built in the late thirties fell

In 1958 the *Golden Gate* lost its observation, seen here at Bakersfield on November 23, 1952 (top). Perhaps Thanksgiving traffic is responsible for the gargantuan consist, which included a pair of off-line Pullmans just ahead of the obs. Bottom left, *Indian Maid,* delivered in 1947 as a 24-duplex-roomette car, in 1964 became an 11-double-bedroom sleeper for *Super Chief* service — seen here at Chicago in the early months of Amtrak. Bottom right, the *Kansas Cityan*'s observation — new in this view — disappeared in 1957. STAN KISTLER, TOP; PETER TILP, BOTTOM LEFT; SANTA FE RAILWAY, BOTTOM RIGHT

before Santa Fe's anti-obs policy: the *San Diegan*'s in 1956, the *Kansas Cityan/Chicagoan*'s in 1957. In a program carried out in 1960 and 1962, nine coach-observations and two parlor-observations, along with twenty-nine Indian-named sleepers, were rebuilt into 48- and 44-seat coaches. Two years later, another major rebuild program converted the dozen *Indian*-series 24-duplex-roomette sleepers (Pullman-Standard, 1947) to 11-bedroom cars for the *Super Chief.* The work, costing more than $1 million, was done at The Pullman Company's Calumet Shops. The rebuilt cars entered service May 10.

Also in 1964 came entirely new equipment: twenty-four Hi-Level cars for *El Capitan,* releasing enough of the 1956 Hi-Levels to give three or four to each *San Francisco Chief* consist on May 4, just one month short of the train's tenth anniversary. This had become a very heavy train in the early 1960's, up to eighteen cars not counting head-end, so this infusion of Hi-Levels was particularly welcome.

The new cars were essentially duplicates of the existing fleet. The only changes were miniscule refinements: an illuminated Lucite handrail along the curved stairway betwen levels, indentations in the backs of the reclining coach seats for more leg room, an extra wash basin in the ladies' lounge. Of the twenty-four cars, twelve were 68-seaters, with a stairway at one end leading to lower-level access to the adjoining car, and twelve were 72-seaters, with both end doors at upper level. This dozen were designed with an end stairwell in place and a floor built over it, so they could readily be converted to step-down cars.

That Santa Fe would make this substantial a capital commitment to new equipment in 1964 was remarkable, but no more so than its ongoing attention to promotion, advertising, and careful, conscious maintenance of service standards. Santa Fe's advertising department, which dates back to 1895, has long been of scope unusual for a railroad. Organized along the lines of an ad agency, it employs copywriters, layout men, display designers, market analysts, and mechanical production men. In 1952, for instance, the railroad's message appeared in fifteen national magazines and 455 daily and 650 weekly newspapers, and on billboards, radio, and television. Travel folders and booklets distributed numbered 176,000, travel posters 40,000, wall calendars 450,000, and pocket calendars 600,000. More than 3,000 window displays were set up.

In 1957, passenger service was one of four thrusts of the advertising program, all under the general theme of "Always on the Move Toward a Better Way." National magazines carried four-color, double-page spreads touting the Hi-Level *El Cap,* a train particularly appropriate to the general message of innovation. "There's so much to *See* on the San Francisco Chief" bannered ads on the bottom half of two facing pages, an unusual format well suited to present the horizontality of a railroad car.

Perhaps most interesting were the graphically understated full-page ads headlined "The Super Chief Feeling." The text read, "If you have ever been a part of the Super Chief crowd, you know." Its message continued, "There's a feeling of belonging. A sense of personal satisfaction that is unobtainable anywhere else (except, perhaps, on an ocean-going luxury liner). The *Super* is, of course, not the least expensive way to go. But we think you'll agree the extra fare is worth it . . . just to know the *Super Chief* feeling." This ad bears a more than passing resemblance to the snooty butler who touted the *Santa Fe de-Luxe* years earlier.

"Good service" meetings, which were held all during the fifties and right up through 1966, were another positive factor in the continuing excellence of Santa Fe's passenger trains. In 1965, these gatherings, by then called "Chico's Better Service and Sales Pow-Wows," were held at twenty different on-line points. This nine-state, six-week tour of the system reached about five thousand Santa Fe employees involved directly or indirectly with passenger operations: sales personnel, ticket or reservation clerks, train crews, and maintenance personnel.

Each year had its own slogan. In 1960 it was "Keep a face in every window," in 1961 "Find the hidden passenger," in 1962 "Sell . . . Serve . . . Satisfy."

The meetings promoted the Santa Fe tradition of courtesy and friendliness, kept employees informed on developments, and solicited their suggestions. (This last was no empty gesture; in 1964, dining- and lounge-car employees offered forty-two suggestions, of which twenty-eight were adopted.)

In 1964, the *San Francisco Chief* received Hi-Level coaches — released from *El Cap* by delivery of twenty-four new cars. These hand-me-down Hi-Levels are part of an equipment display at Fisherman's Wharf in San Francisco (above), and in the consist of this westbound *San Francisco Chief* in Abo Canyon, New Mexico (left).
SANTA FE RAILWAY

A novel idea pursued through the early and mid sixties was the "Travel Tips Program." Employees were encouraged to submit names and addresses of people they knew who were planning trips which might be made by Santa Fe. The railroad's sales staff would follow up these leads and, if a trip resulted, prize points—one for every mile of travel—would be awarded the tipster employee. Prizes included luggage, clocks, watches, and sporting goods. In 1961, for example, 1,765 tips were submitted; 876 were converted to travel, yielding revenue of $127,567.

New equipment, innovative programs including bargain fares and budget meals, plenty of advertising, "beating the drums for courtesy and more sales" at the better service meetings: In the middle sixties all this seemed to be working, as passenger revenues increased every year but one. In January 1967 Santa Fe began honoring BankAmericards and Midwest Bank Cards and touted other innovations: gift certificates, 20-percent off-season fare reductions, reduced meal costs under a dining-club program, family fares extended to all days of the week, "Chico" all-expense-paid tours. Dining-car-department good service meetings went forward, where Ross E. Chappell, general passenger traffic manager, could say: "Because of our confidence in the future of long-distance rail travel, we're here to find and effect new methods to serve the train traveling public."

But as the months wore on 1967 would not prove a good year for Santa Fe passenger trains. Instead, it would prove a very black year, the year the bubble burst. On January 1 John S. Reed had become president (taking over from Ernest S. Marsh, who stayed on as chairman of the board and chief operating officer). To Reed fell the unenviable task on October 4 of issuing a statement as shocking as it was inevitable. Santa Fe was finally throwing in the towel.

Top, the *Super Chief* (left) and *El Capitan* (right) depart Dearborn Station, Chicago, on June 18, 1966. Bottom, on August 16, 1962, in Pasadena, California, the *Super,* sans obs, still displays a drumhead. Facing page: Just two days later, a pair of PA's haul a lengthy *San Diegan* through Del Mar, California. PETER TILP, TOP; STAN KISTLER, BOTTOM AND FACING PAGE

SANTA FE

Loss of mail contracts was a major cause for Santa Fe's massive 1968 discontinuance. Top, eastbound mail No. 4 arrives Kansas City terminal on October 30, 1966, when the Post Office was still a good customer. Bottom, also at Kansas City, No. 8, the *Fast Mail,* catches the late afternoon light on April 10, 1965. STEVE PATTERSON. Facing page: Santa Fe was an early practitioner of containerized mail, using cars such as this one, photographed at Barstow, California, in December 1962; others like it are in the consists of the *Chicagoan* at Kansas City in October 1966 and the westbound *San Francisco Chief,* emerging from Franklin Canyon Tunnel at Christie, California, on January 17, 1967. W. C. WHITTAKER, ROBERT J. WAYNER COLLECTION, TOP LEFT; STEVE PATTERSON, TOP RIGHT; VICTOR HAND, BOTTOM

The gist of the ominous document, titled "Future Passenger Train Service on the Santa Fe," was that "present-day circumstances warrant a reappraisal of the size of our passenger operations." Specifically, this would mean the retention of the *Super Chief, El Capitan, San Francisco Chief, Texas Chief,* and *San Diegan.* Everything else would go: *Fast Mail, Grand Canyon, Kansas City Chief, Kansas Cityan, Chicagoan, Tulsan, Oil Flyer, El Pasoan,* half a dozen unnamed local services, and—the most stunning victim—the *Chief.*

Reed cited as the most immediate cause of this action the United States Post Office Department's notification of Santa Fe on September 6 that, within one month, all but two Railway Post Office cars would be removed from AT&SF trains. "Nearly $35 million of annual mail revenue, the backbone of our passenger trains, will no longer be available to help support these trains," according to Reed.

An even more basic problem was the preciptious 17.3 percent drop in passenger revenues in the first eight months of 1967 compared to the same period in 1966—a devastating decline, particularly considering the modest but almost unbroken revenue growth of about 2 percent annually throughout the sixties. Reed summed up his inarguable case this way: "Since 1946 we have spent $136 million for cars and locomotives used in passenger train service. Several thousand miles of continuous welded rail have been installed to produce a better ride and reduce maintenance costs. An aggressive TV, magazine, and newspaper advertising campaign, bank credit cards, One Price Tickets, Family and Off-Season Fares—all have been employed to attract patronage. We have placed special emphasis on

U.S. MAIL

86
SANTA FE
PAXTON

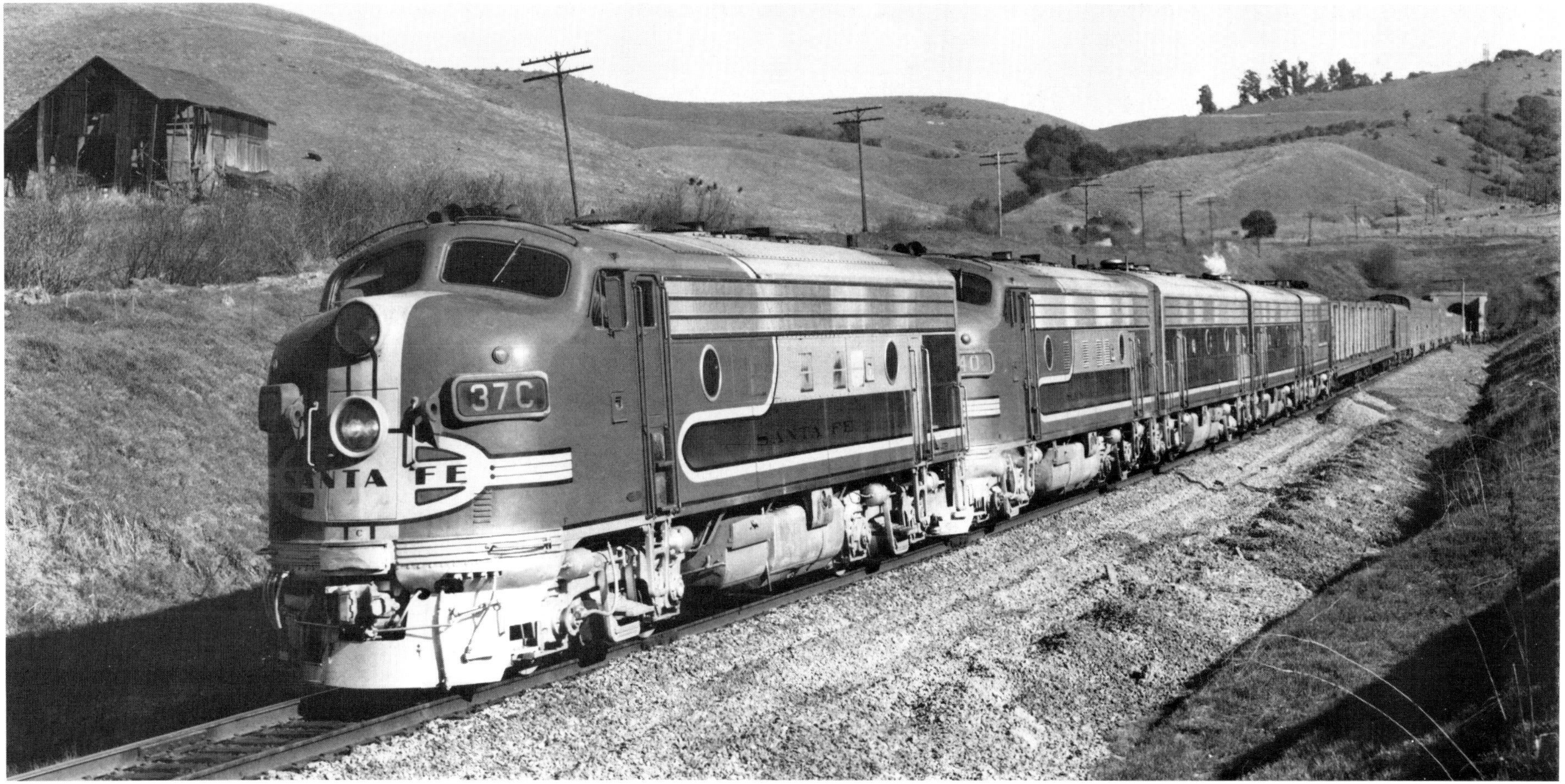

courtesy and service by educational seminars, incentive programs, and the like. Equipment maintenance and cleanliness coupled with good food service have been paramount.

"Santa Fe has not abandoned the traveling public—travelers show an increased preference to drive or fly."

Of course, the Interstate Commerce Commission got its chance to agree or disagree with Santa Fe's logic—and it did both. To the majority of the trains on the discontinuance petition, the ICC gave its blessing, but in a few places it balked. Thus some unlikely trains made it right up to Amtrak: Nos. 191/190 and 200/201, the unnamed La Junta-Denver connection for the *Super/El Cap;* Nos. 211 and 212, the Kansas City-Tulsa *Tulsan;* and Nos. 23 and 24, formerly the *Grand Canyon* but shorn of that name and reduced to a consist as short as two cars, with no diner or lounge, in the winter of 1967-68. (After the ICC's refusal to allow discontinuance, Santa Fe restored a lounge and lunch-counter diner.)

But 1968 saw some famous names leave the timetable,

Top left, No. 23, formerly the *Grand Canyon,* is just two coaches and a baggage car on May 13, 1968, traversing Raton Pass. Top right, No. 191/190, the Denver-La Junta *Super Chief* connection, survived the 1968 bloodbath; here it leaves Denver in July 1969. Bottom, the last eastbound *Chief* rolls over Raton Pass. The date: May 14, 1968. VICTOR HAND, TOP LEFT AND BOTTOM; KARL ZIMMERMANN, TOP RIGHT. Facing page: Even in the discouraging sixties, Santa Fe continued to put its best foot forward through newspaper and magazine advertising and colorful brochures, such as this one. PETER TILP COLLECTION

The Alco PA's were closely identified with Santa Fe passenger railroading, and their demise — which occurred near the time of the great train-offs of 1968 — further deepened the gloom. These views are from March 3, 1968, when PA's Nos. 58 and 67 made a farewell fantrip. Top left, morning haze lingers into early afternoon as Extra 58 West strides onto the long steel trestle at Muir, California. Top right, with the special paused at Stockton for lunch, the hogger aboard PA 58 had this view of F7 37C leading No. 2, the *San Francisco Chief.* Bottom, east of Muir, on the trip's return leg, the special — now Extra 67 East — makes a photo run-by for Alco admirers. The relatively short consist — seven cars, streamlined and heavyweight mixed — shows that not all the faithful were paying attention. TED BENSEN

At Suwanee, New Mexico, under summer skies that presage violent thundershowers, five F's roar west with No. 23, the *Grand Canyon.* In this view from 1967, the train is still respectable, with four coaches, a diner, a lounge, and three sleepers — a smooth-sided gray AT&SF car, a Rio Grande, and one in Illinois Central dress. ROGER COOK

most notably the *Chief,* on May 13. On April 18, the westbound *Kansas City Chief* (whose eastbound counterpart had gone in 1957), the Dallas-Kansas City *Kansas Cityan* remnant, and the *Chicagoan* had died. April 9 had seen the end of the RDC-equipped *El Pasoan*. Lesser lights were victims too: the *Fast Mail,* the connection to the Grand Canyon from the main line at Williams, Arizona, and the *Oil Flyer* among them.

Of course, even after these discontinuances the Santa Fe ran arguably the best train in the country, the *Super/El Cap,* plus two other superbly maintained long-distance services, the *San Francisco Chief* and the *Texas Chief.* This latter train inherited the *Chief's* Big Domes and so was better equipped than ever before. In the summer of 1969, the last when the *Super Chief* and *El Capitan* were run in two sections, the *Super* was once again all-Pullman—for the first summer since the trains' consolidation in 1958.

That the Santa Fe's remaining streamliners were well run right up to the end led to widespread speculation that AT&SF would not join Amtrak but would continue to run its own streamliners in the style to which it had become accustomed. However, on April 16, 1971, the National Railroad Passenger Corporation offered Santa Fe a final contract and, four days later, the railroad signed. Ten days after that it was out of the passenger business, but not without mixed emotions, as suggested by John Reed's statement:

"Beyond a doubt this decision was one of the most difficult that Santa Fe management has ever had to face. For over a hundred years our passenger service has been our showcase. . . . One does not give up such proud traditions easily and without a great deal of study. On the other hand, mounting financial losses from providing poorly patronized passenger service have become an intolerable drain on our resources and have threatened the security of all of us." So Santa Fe joined Amtrak, paying joining fees of more than $21 million over a three-year period.

Amtrak would continue the *Super Chief/El Capitan,* the *Texas Chief,* and two *San Diegan* round trips, adding the Los Angeles-San Diego leg of a triweekly through train to Seattle in place of the third. Santa Fe's other trains, including the *San Francisco Chief,* would be dropped. "I have told the Amtrak people," Reed continued, "that we will work closely with them to carry on our traditional service and have said that as long as these standards can be maintained under Amtrak we are willing to lend the use of our traditional names, such as Super Chief, Texas Chief, and El Capitan, to the surviving trains."

Amtrak purchased an enormous number of Santa Fe

Santa Fe went in for second-generation passenger diesels far more heavily than any other long-distance passenger hauler — yet another example of the road's stubborn commitment to passenger excellence in the darkening days of the sixties. In 1966 came ten U28CG hood units from General Electric — termed "dual service." In 1967 and '68 came two kinds of cowl units — nine 3600-horsepower FP45's from EMD and six 3000-horsepower U30CG's from GE. Left, on June 29, 1968, running independently again for the summer rush, first 17, the *Super Chief,* is FP45-hauled west of La Junta, Colorado. No. 105 was carrying green for the following second section — the *El Cap.* Below, just the month before — on May 13 — the consists are combined and led by a pair of FP45's eastbound over Raton Pass. STEVE PATTERSON, LEFT; VICTOR HAND, BELOW. Facing page: Top left, Santa Fe poses a brand-new FP45 fleet; bottom left, No. 15, the southbound *Texas Chief,* is hauled through Temple, Texas, by a U30CG bracketed by U28CG's in this summer 1969 view; right, three U28CG's haul the *Texas Chief* through the Arbuckle Mountains of Oklahoma. SANTA FE RAILWAY, RIGHT AND TOP LEFT; STEVE PATTERSON, BOTTOM LEFT

104
107
103

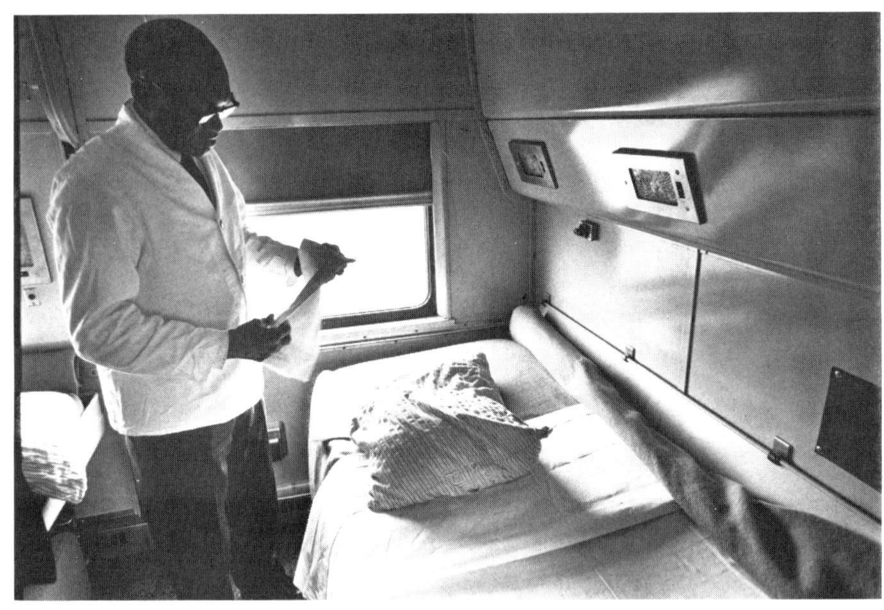

Facing page: The demise of the *San Francisco Chief.* Left, just ten days before the end, sleeping-car porter Frank Peppers (top) and waiter C. D. Miller (bottom) still ply their time-honored trades aboard No. 1, the westbound *San Francisco Chief.* Right, the final eastbound train slips out of Riverbank, California, on April 30, 1971 — put out to pasture by Amtrak. F7's ruled trains 1 and 2 right up to the last runs, when they bowed to cowl units. TED BENSEN. Right: Two views of Amtrak's *Southwest Limited* at Seligman, Arizona, on August 10, 1978 (top) and January 26, 1979 (bottom). STEVE PATTERSON

passenger cars: nearly 450, well over a third of Amtrak's entire fleet. Amtrak took ninety baggage cars and four baggage dorms, seventy-one sleepers in the *Pine, Palm, Regal, Indian,* and *Blue* series, fourteen buffet-lounges of four different types, 140 coaches, thirty-seven lunch-counter and 36-seat conventional diners (including six *Super Chief* cars), the six Pleasure Domes, and the entire Hi-Level fleet, numbering seventy-nine including the six low-level baggage-dormitories with Hi-Level adapters.

Notable omissions were the Big Domes. Auto-Train snapped up thirteen of these (all but one, which AT&SF held for its own use), along with six *Regal*-series sleepers. Twenty-six 52-seat coaches, including the Budd prototype from 1936, No. 3070, went to the New Jersey Department of Transportation for commuter service. The ready market for Santa Fe's passenger fleet offered yet another confirmation of the superb maintenance the cars had always received.

In Amtrak's early years, the *Super Chief/El Cap* was left intact with a reverence accorded no other train. Though *El Capitan* was dropped from the name in 1973, its Hi-Level cars remained, as did the 600-series *Super Chief* diners and the Pleasure Dome lounge cars. For three months in the summer of 1973, Amtrak even revived the *Chief,* on its old schedule and carrying its traditional numbers, 19 and 20.

But as plans were being laid for the next summer season, things turned sour. Amtrak apparently projected two-section operation of the *Super;* one of the sections was to have a capacity of three hundred and just a single 36-seat diner. This, according to John

Diesel disposition: Four PA's went to Delaware & Hudson in December 1967; half of these are seen here hauling the *Laurentian* south at Coopersville, New York. Some F7's went to Mexico's Chihuahua Pacifico, such as CH-P 402, seen here at Cuauhtemoc, Chihuahua. Both PA's and F show their "Warbonneted" heritage clearly. KARL ZIMMERMANN, TOP; JOE McMILLAN, BOTTOM

Facing page, right: No. 3087 (top) was among the twenty-six coaches purchased by New Jersey Department of Transportation (and is seen here at New Haven, Connecticut, in January 1975). Budd prototype 3070 was also in that lot. *Forward,* the prototype lightweight sleeper, ended life as dormitory 3473 (middle); it was off the roster before Amtrak's inception. But many AT&SF cars did go to Amtrak, including these sleepers in *Super Chief* service in September 1973, at Flagstaff, Arizona (bottom). DONALD T. HAYWARD, JR., ROBERT J. WAYNER COLLECTION, TOP; PETER TILP, MIDDLE; TED BENSEN, BOTTOM. Right: Santa Fe kept some cars, including a Big Dome, for use in company trains — such as this directors' special, seen at Romeoville, New Mexico, on April 23, 1985 (top), and at Wootton Ranch, Colorado, two days previous (bottom). JOHN LUCAS, TOP; CHIP SHERMAN, BOTTOM

Reed, would "lower the quality of service to a level hardly recognizable by those accustomed to past Santa Fe standards." Reed went on to point out, in an announcement dated March 7, 1974, that Santa Fe had "expressly reserved the right to withdraw permission to use the Chief names should the quality of service provided by Amtrak on the trains so identified no longer reflect credit on Santa Fe." So Reed told Roger Lewis, president of Amtrak, to drop the names "Super Chief" and "Texas Chief"; thus were born the *Southwest Limited* and the *Lone Star*.

Other than the rails on which they rode, there grew to be less and less connection between these trains and their heritage. The warbonneted F's which continued to haul the trains in Amtrak's first years disappeared, giving way to SDP40F's and later F40PH's in red, blue, and platinum mist. In the Amtrak service cuts of 1979, the *Lone Star* disappeared entirely. On November 30, 1980, Amtrak's Superliners—which owe their design to Santa Fe's Hi-Levels—replaced the Pleasure Domes and Hi-Levels themselves on the *Super*.

Happily, the story of Santa Fe's streamliners has an upbeat ending. Service standards on Amtrak had improved sufficiently that, with the October 28, 1984, time change, Amtrak allowed the *Southwest Limited* to become the *Southwest Chief*. In the resurrection of the "Chief" name, and in the small streamliner fleet Santa Fe has retained for company use—a Big Dome, ex-*Super Chief* diner No. 600, six *Regal*-series sleepers, a club-lounge—a glimmer remains of the lightweight *Chiefs* and their tribesmen on the Santa Fe.

Acknowledgments

Among the great pleasures of assembling a book is the outpouring of help received from many quarters. *Santa Fe Streamliners* has been no exception. Beginning with the railroad itself, an army of contributors has marched with me down the long road to completion of this project.

At Santa Fe's public relations department, both Bob Gehrt and Jeff Newton have been endlessly hospitable and helpful, opening up for me archives, library, and files. Joe McMillan, another Santa Fe man but acting more in an unofficial capacity as friend, lent support.

Peter Tilp participated in many ways; he shared information, did research, read the manuscript, and provided photographs and other invaluable material from his collection. Bob Wayner also was generous in the same ways.

A book like this succeeds or fails on its photographs, and here again I have benefited from the Santa Fe's cooperation. Another major contributor was Stan Kistler, who generously shared a significant number of his dramatic images. I am also grateful to Gordon Bassett for opening his collection, and to the Denver Public Library for the Otto Perry photographs, from the Western History Collection.

To Steve Patterson go thanks for the cover picture, as well as photos used inside. Thanks also to the other contributing photographers: Dick Kindig, Ted Bensen, Victor Hand, Bob Collins, Roger Cook, Chip Sherman, John Lucas, and Fred Matthews.

I had other allies. Robert Gordon's sharp editorial pen worked over my prose. Varda Amdur designed the cover. Larry Blizard, with Santa Fe's blessing, helped Chico write chapter titles in the sand.

"Remembering the Super Chief" appeared in a slightly different version as "A Miracle of Rare Device" in the June 15, 1971, issue of *National Review*; permission to use it here is appreciated.

A bibliography follows, but I point out as having been of special value the late Stan Repp's *The Super Chief . . . Train of the Stars*, Fred Frailey's *A Quarter Century of Santa Fe Consists*, and Robert Wayner's *Car Names, Numbers, and Consists*.

—*K. Z.*

PHOTO BY LAUREL ZIMMERMANN

About the Author

Santa Fe Streamliners is Karl Zimmermann's tenth book about trains. His first — *CZ: The Story of the California Zephyr* — was published in 1972. Other books include *The Milwaukee Road Under Wire, Erie Lackawanna East, A Decade of D&H, The Remarkable GG1, Paradise Regained: A South African Steam Diary*, and *Amtrak at Milepost 10*.

With Roger Cook, Zimmermann wrote *The Western Maryland Railway: Fireballs and Black Diamonds* and with Ed Nowak *Ed Nowak's New York Central*. Zimmermann has written over one hundred articles on a wide variety of subjects for *Trains*, *Railfan*, *International Railway Traveler*, *Locomotive & Railway Preservation*, *The New York Times* Travel Section, *Americana Magazine*, *Amtrak Express*, *Historic Preservation*, The New York *Post* Travel Section, *Bon Appetit*, and others. He is a contributing editor to *Passenger Train Journal*.

A 1965 graduate of Princeton University with a master's degree in English from New York University, Karl Zimmermann lives in Dobbs Ferry, New York, with wife Laurel and daughters Jennifer and Emily.

Bibliography

Beebe, Lucius and Clegg, Charles. *The Trains We Rode, Volume I*. Berkeley, Calif.: Howell-North Books, 1965.

Dolzall, Gary W. "Shadows of Things That Have Been," Trains, XLIII (December 1982), 40-45.

Dubin, Arthur D. *Some Classic Trains*. Milwaukee: Kalmbach Publishing Company, 1964.

Frailey, Fred W. *A Quarter Century of Santa Fe Consists*. Godfrey, Ill.: RPC Publications, 1974.

Grattan, Virginia L. *Mary Colter: Builder Upon the Red Earth*. Flagstaff, Ariz.: Northland Press, 1980.

Harper, Jared V. *Santa Fe's Raton Pass*. Dallas: Kachina Press, 1983.

Herbert, Charles W. "The Fred Harvey Story," *Arizona Highways*, (June 1968), 10-11, 30-34.

McCall, John. *Santa Fe's Early Diesel Daze: 1935-1953*. Dallas: Kachina Press, 1980.

Pinkepank, Jerry A. *The Second Diesel Spotter's Guide*. Milwaukee: Kalmbach Books, 1973.

Railway Age

Reed, Robert C. *The Streamline Era*. San Marino, Calif.: Golden West Books, 1975.

Repp, Stan. "The Story of the Super Chief," *Trains*, XXII (May 1962), 30-41.

Repp, Stan. *The Super Chief . . . Train of the Stars*. San Marino, Calif.: Golden West Books, 1980.

The Santa Fe Magazine

Wayner, Robert J. *Car Names, Numbers, and Consists*. New York: Wayner Publications, 1972.